The Nervous New Owner's Guide to
Angora Rabbits

by Suzie Sugrue

Printed in the United States of America.

ISBN: 978-0-578-07177-0

Santa Fe, New Mexico
www.hareandthereproductions.com

Cover Photos:
(front)

Skeins of handspun, 100% angora yarn. Photo courtesy of Katie Musante, High
Desert Fiberworks.

A sweater knitted from angora, silk and wool. Photo by author.

The very handsome angora buck, Hop Smudge Sundae. Photo courtesy of
Chris Morgan, Woolybuns Rabbitry.

Maggie Tipping and her English angora rabbit, Cocoa Bean. Photo courtesy of
Maggie Tipping.

(back)

An angora kit takes a look at the camera. Photo courtesy of Katie Musante,
High Desert Fiberworks.

Bunny in a basket. Photo courtesy of Christine Durkin, We Spin Angora.

To Randy,
for his steadfast support and love.
He said I could do it. And he was right!

And to
the Thursday Night Crafters
Anna, Carmela, Marina, Lisa, Gina, Lisa, Pat, Carol,
our newest addition, Erika, and the seldom-seen Eleanore
for wonderful continuity, diversity, conversation,
inspiration, food and friendship.

Contents

A Rabbit Tale

One fine fall day, my sister and her husband took me along with them to the Taos Wool Festival, which takes place each year on the first weekend in October. The festival brings avid spinners, knitters, felters, weavers and general crafty-type folks together with those who offer tools, books, supplies, workshops and maintain the herds of animals from which we harvest such fibery goodness. It's a feast for the senses.

My first year in attendance, I ran around like the proverbial "kid in a candy store". It was such an exciting, energizing environment! (I may even have jumped up and down a few times.) I spent a lot of money and learned a lot. From that time on, the end of summer could cause me no dismay, as I knew the Taos Wool Festival would be just around the corner.

But something special happened on the third year of my attending the festival. (Could it be that three really IS a charmed number?) By then, I'd been knitting and spinning up a storm. Folks hardly saw me without some kind of project in my hands. And I really wanted a fiber herd. Of course, this desire was impractical. My husband and I, along with our two kids and multiple dogs, cats, etc., lived (and still do) in a suburban house in Santa Fe. I'd managed to talk my family into having a small flock of laying chickens to live in our side yard. That had turned out well. But sheep? Alpacas? Llamas, for goodness sake?!?!?! I knew there was one fiber animal that might be acceptable to my family and fit within the limits of my home's urban setting.

Rabbits.

Furry rabbits.

(No, I'd never owned rabbits prior to then. Are you kidding? Who owns rabbits? Dogs, sure. Cats, of course. Chickens – a little unusual, but it made sense once the fresh eggs started arriving. But rabbits?... never thought of it.)

I'd seen them at the Taos festival in previous years. This year, I thought, I would take a closer look, ask questions, get a feel for what keeping an angora or two might involve... You know -- employ a calm, measured, rational approach to what might become a new undertaking.

My sister and I went to the festival that year, as always, ready to run around the gathering of vendors in an excited frenzy. The colors! The textures! The amazing garments, skeins of yarn and rugs! We didn't make it halfway around the park before I came upon an angora rabbit breeder and her wares. Miles of spun angora. Batts like clouds in the sky. Delicate treasures knit from the softest yarn you've ever touched. Rabbits for sale. I asked to hold one.

You can guess what happened next.

Yep. I took one home.

Long sigh...

If you've picked up this book, then you've either experienced that moment or you want to. Either way, you might as well start stocking up on timothy hay. (What's timothy hay? We'll get to that...) Once you've held and stroked one of these rabbits, if you are at all of a mind to own one, you will find a way to make it work.

I brought mine home that day, in a big cardboard box. He was promptly set up for the night in a wire dog crate, given a bowl of water, a handful of pellets and a promise that I would figure out the rest as soon as I could. I named him Winston. By the next morning, panic had set in.

What does he need? Where will I house him? What if he gets matted? How will the dogs react? What does he eat? Am I really supposed to pick him up and PULL his hair out??? Eeeeeeeek! The breeder had given me a single sheet of paper with basic directions for rabbit care. I must have read it thirty times. It wasn't enough information to help me calm down. Not nearly enough. I felt woefully ignorant.

Winston looked at me from within the dog crate. He wiggled his nose. He flopped down on his side and stuck out a foot. He was unconcerned.

What did he know that I didn't, to be so calm?

He knew this: that time, discussions with other angora owners, trial and error and online research would take care of all my questions. And my angst. And eventually, him. And fourteen more just like him. (But that's a story for another time...)

I sure could have used an introductory book in those first months. One to hold in my hands, to clutch and page through while in the throes of worry. I didn't need a comprehensive tome; I had no intentions of becoming a pro. I needed a basic how-to-take-care-of-your-angora-rabbit-and-here-are-some-things-that-will-happen-so-don't-get-too-excited-about-them kind of guide.

There wasn't one.

For angora rabbits, that is.

For other rabbits? Sure. Books galore! Websites aplenty! But not for the very special, fiber-producing animal I'd brought home. Angora rabbits have a different set of needs than the short-haired variety of rabbit most folks own.

I wrote this guidebook to provide you with the information that I would have wanted to have myself, on that very first day I brought Winston home. Or, had I been just a tad more patient and rational, that I should have obtained in the weeks *before* I brought him home. I offer it to you now, along with my best wishes.

Here I am, holding my first angora rabbit, Winston. You can almost see the thoughts circling my mind... "Here he is! Goodness, he's cute. But what have I gotten myself into?!?!?!"

First Things First

How to Find
Your Angora Rabbit

If you haven't already brought home an angora, your first step is finding one. This may sound like a simple task. I can assure you... it isn't. But with a little patience and tenacity, it can be done. Think of it as a treasure hunt! Start here:

- Look for a **local breeder** by searching online, asking at area feed stores (they know who's buying rabbit feed!) and checking in with 4-H groups. If you are very, very lucky, you will find a reputable owner with extra rabbits or baby bunnies (referred to as "kits") that lives within driving distance.

- Attend **fiber festivals**. Angora rabbit owners, if they are in business, will sell at fiber festivals whenever possible. They know that attendees come specifically to locate and purchase fiber, yarns and animals for sale. When you find vendors with available rabbits, review the offerings quickly and make your choice(s). Angora vendors often sell out, and often on the very first day. I'm so sure of this avenue for locating angora rabbits that if you don't find fiber rabbits at a major fiber festival, I promise to eat my felted hat.

Sherry Redden, of Redden Rabbitry in Sargents, CO, sets up her booth at the Taos Wool Festival.

• Check at **county and state fairs and ARBA rabbit shows.** Many folks show angora rabbits. In fact, there are many more people involved in showing angora rabbits than in keeping them as fiber pets. Luckily for us fiber enthusiasts, breeders do occasionally come up with a rabbit ineligible to show because of a color, size or attribute flaw (like a white toenail or bent, floppy ear). In these situations, breeders are more than happy to find these "losers" a good home. Like yours!

- Nothing beats **online angora discussion groups** for information. The internet has become the ultimate networking tool for angora rabbit lovers. Any breeder with a litter of kits will post the information online, along with adorable pictures, in order to reach as wide an audience as possible. You will also find folks looking to rehome animals and announcements regarding upcoming litters. Members of online groups are happy to direct you to breeders, events and other resources in your area.

- Don't forget your **local animal shelter or rabbit rescue group**. Rabbits are generally difficult for shelters to adopt out, as their appeal is not as wide as that of dogs and cats. An angora rabbit, with the additional time and effort involved in its care, can be a real challenge to rehome. Shelters will be overjoyed that you have contacted them. To look beyond your local area, check the listings on petfinder.com, a national clearinghouse for animal shelters and rescue groups. A note of caution: rescue groups have much more stringent requirements for adoptive owners than animal shelters do. Some will not release an animal if it is to be housed outside or used as "livestock". Be honest about your reasons for wanting an angora rabbit. It's an education for them and you will feel better having presented yourself honestly. If it doesn't work out with the rescue group, continue searching for an angora through the other resources mentioned above.

Once you are ready to purchase a rabbit, visit the rabbitry or shelter. You will want to insure the animal has been well taken care of, that it is healthy and is worth the purchase price or adoption fee. If a visit is not possible, you can still get a good picture of the rabbitry by asking a lot of questions. Try the following topics:

- What kind of **housing** is in use? Are the cages/hutches generally clean, airy and well kept? Or are they filth-encrusted and overcrowded? How does the breeder protect animals from extremes of weather? Do the animals receive regular opportunities to **exercise**?

- Are parents, siblings and/or other rabbits in **good health**? Do you see well-kept coats, feet and teeth? Ask to handle a few to get a sense of their personalities and suitability for your needs.

- Can the breeder provide you with **references**, preferably for previous customers or someone involved in the fiber or rabbit community? Don't be shy. Ask away. Anyone who cares about their animals and their reputation as a breeder will appreciate your desire to make inquiries.

A rabbit awaits pickup by her new owner at the Taos Wool Festival.

ꓷecision Makinᴑ...
Age, Gender, Utility, Numbers, Breeds, Coloring and a Note on Breeding

Age

There's nothing more appealing than a baby bunny. Kits are indescribably adorable. If you see a group of tiny, fuzzy, wiggling rabbits you will be hard-pressed to resist their charms. Take your time, enjoy watching them and maybe even pick out one or two. Realize, however, that breeders cannot release an animal to a new owner until *well after* they are weaned at 8 weeks. These tiny cuties will be offered for sale in the age range of 12 to 16 weeks – by which time kits are feeding independently and are about halfway to their adult size. But kits are not your only option.

Breeders in the business of selling rabbits offer young adults -- from 6 months to a year old -- throughout the year. They may also offer an adult -- any rabbit over 12 months of age -- if additional space is needed in the rabbitry or the adult rabbit does not exhibit specific characteristics which the breeder is working toward in a breeding program. You have a choice then, of deciding on either a newborn rabbit, a young adult or an adult to bring into your home. There are pros and cons to each.

The advantage of a baby or young adult rabbit is that it will be very comfortable in your presence -- provided you handle it often and well during its first few months with you. The disadvantage is that its soft, downy coat will require extra monitoring and grooming efforts to keep it matt-free. And until its adult coat comes in, around one year of age, you won't be sure of the color or "hand" (the feel) of its wool. Many angora owners love the baby coat, though. Its super-fine softness is worth the effort involved in its care and gathering.

A few of my friends enjoying the cute faces from a litter of angora kits.

With an adult rabbit, you will know exactly what you are getting in the way of size, coat and temperament. The disadvantage with an adult rabbit is that it will not know you. Time, patience and effort will be required to develop a comfortable relationship between the two of you. If the previous owner handled the rabbit a great deal (and well), the process of creating that bond will go much more smoothly. And indeed, all rabbits have their own unique personalities. Some will be ready to engage with you as soon as their environment stabilizes. Others will remain aloof, depending upon their individual temperament. One advantage of choosing an older rabbit is that you can make your preferences known and have the breeder/previous owner advise you on the best match.

Susan Helgeson is delighted with her new buddy, Zorro. He's a German/English X buck from Angora Moon Rabbitry in Deming, NM.

The Nervous New Owner's Guide to **Angora Rabbits**

Gender

As with cats and dogs, there's a running debate about which of the sexes makes a better fiber pet. Each gender has its enthusiasts. In my experience, gender does not guarantee a particular personality or temperament. I recommend choosing your rabbit based on whether you are drawn to it, rather than on a predetermined decision to acquire a particular gender. However, there are some generalities which I think are worth communicating.

Bucks (males) tend to be more interested in their surroundings, affectionate with people and even-tempered -- especially if neutered. In fact, neutered males are often recommended as the best choice for new owners, especially those interested in a fiber pet. On the down side, bucks can spray urine when their environment excites them. The area surrounding their cages must be protected to prevent staining of nearby walls, stored items and rabbits. Bucks have a reputation of fighting with each other. They can inflict serious damage with their sharp teeth and powerful hind legs. You will want to house and exercise bucks individually or in the company of females, not in the company of other bucks.

Does (females) are generally less affectionate, cleaner (no spraying!), more temperamental and smaller than their male counterparts. They provide the option of making more rabbits! (Hmmm... is that a positive or a negative?) Does exercise and live together quite contentedly. They commonly bond with another doe or buck. You'll see this coupling described as "a bonded pair". Does will also willingly share a cage with male or female siblings, especially if they have done so since birth. Feel free to leave a group of does (and one buck, if you like) unsupervised for long stretches of time. Once they've determined their dominance hierarchy, they won't fight. You'll see them chase each other around in play and then a few minutes later, lie down side by side to rest, groom each other and "chill out" together.

Utility

What you do with your rabbits (i.e. "utility") will affect the cost of acquiring them. The cost for an angora rabbit ranges from free (if a breeder cannot show their rabbit, someone decides to retire from the business or there's an OOPS litter and you're lucky enough to be within driving distance) to upwards of $300. Reputable, pedigreed foundation stock, especially for the somewhat rare German Angoras, will cost more than that. Yes, per rabbit! Does that surprise you?

Keep in mind this rabbit is not a companion animal. This rabbit is an investment. Your investment will offer its returns in the form of angora wool -- a useful and marketable product. And in some cases, the returns will be in the form of new rabbits.

Take time to ponder your criteria for getting a rabbit. Are animals a large part of your life? Are you interested in showing or perhaps becoming a breeder? It may not be in the current plan for your rabbit(s), but you may wish to become involved in one or both of these activities in the future. If there's the smallest chance that you will, I recommend you spend the money necessary to obtain pedigreed rabbits from excellent stock. Whether you show, become a breeder or do neither, you'll get great rabbits. And you'll keep your options open in case you want to venture into other activities.

On the other hand, if you're a craft-oriented individual and would enjoy owning a fiber-producing animal, you're more likely in the market for a "wooler" (the term used for a rabbit with unknown lineage, mixed breeding or a disqualification from showing). Woolers are decidedly less expensive than pedigreed rabbits. Their origins and markings are not very important since their utility is related more to the joys of ownership and a harvest of bunny wool. If you decide on a "wooler", look for a healthy animal with a demeanor and coloring that appeals to you.

Who's more proud of this Best of Breed ribbon... Emma Durkin or her chestnut agouti English buck, Jacob?

Numbers

One bunny sounds like a good place to start. One bunny will bond with you and relish your attention. One bunny will need things to do while you are not around (see the description of bunny toys and exercise areas in Part II). One bunny requires a limited outlay of cash for the required set up. One bunny seems reasonable. But one bunny is, after all, just one bunny.

Do bunnies get lonely?

We really don't know. Everyone involved with bunnies has an opinion. As far as I know, no rabbits have spoken up about the issue. But since everyone has an opinion on the matter, I offer mine, based solely on observations and gut feeling.

I think they do.

Spinner and Lizzie, two of my English angora does, snuggle under snow and protective blankets in their shared hutch.

Bunnies relish each other's company. Even when given a great deal of space in which to romp and play (an activity best done with a pal, by the way), they will ultimately lie down and hang out right next to each other. They love to groom each other. You will often hear two described as "a bonded pair". The pair will live companionably in a shared cage, content to have a friend.

Some rabbit owners will be that necessary friend. They are quite willing to shower their single rabbits with petting, treats and active play time. They curl up on the couch with their rabbits to watch movies together. These are unusual rabbit owners. I admire their attentiveness. But they are not like most folks I know, busy with errands, kids, meals, work, school, chores and the additional thousand and one daily items that require attendance. Faced with the distractions of daily life, it might be best to bring home at least two rabbits. They can take care of each other while you are taking care of everything else.

It's easy to get carried away by the appeal of angora rabbits. Don't obtain more than you can reasonably care for. And keep the rest of your household in mind. It might be overwhelming for them if you arrive home one day with eight rabbits. (Not saying I haven't done it. Just saying it might not work for your particular set of circumstances.)

Instead, start slowly. Be conservative. Know that angora rabbits will require more time than you think, especially while you are still a novice. Then later, add more if you want. And subtract if you need to. Eventually you come to the magic place wherein you have sufficient bunnies to meet your fiber (and cute animal) needs but are not overwhelmed by the responsibilities involved.

Breeds

English angora rabbits ("EAs") are the most diminutive of the breeds. Their adult size ranges from 4 to 8 pounds. They produce approximately 4 to 6 oz. of prime fiber per year by shedding, or "blowing" their coats every three months. EAs have fluffs of fur on their head, ears and face – referred to as "furnishings". Their coats are quite soft and downy. Relative to the other breeds, even their guard hair is very fine and there is a smaller proportion of it disbursed throughout their coat. Their coats also have the most crimp, introducing a measure of loft and memory.

Rebecca Gould's English angora, Cocoa Puff, in full coat.

English angoras are friendly and easy to handle. A side benefit of EAs is that due to their unusual looks, they engender great surprise and amusement when introduced to the general public. They also, without doubt, require the greatest amount of time in care as they are fully covered (including on face, feet, ears, bellies and butt area) with fur that needs grooming.

The nitty gritty on EAs: the most unusual, affectionate and smallest of the breeds. EAs produce the best fiber for all-around use due to its lovely crimp, light weight and soft hand. They do, however, require a substantial commitment of time and attention to care for their coats.

French angora rabbits ("FAs" or "Frenchies") look much more like conventional rabbits. They have "clean" faces, feet and butt areas – the result of which is reduced grooming time for the owner. Frenchies produce approximately 4 to 8 oz. of fiber per year. Their wool has greater weight, is a bit more coarse and has a larger share of guard hairs than that of the EAs. It spins up into a yarn with greater density (though still light in comparison to other fibers) and produces a very dramatic "halo".

Zia, one of the my Frenchies. She rules the herd!

French angoras blow (i.e. shed or molt) their coats with the same frequency as English. However, there are a few French lines that do not shed their fibers as readily as the rabbit matures. They require shearing for a wool harvest. French angoras are in the middle range regarding size, weighing in at 8 to 10 pounds at full growth.

The nitty gritty on Frenchies: ideal for new angora owners due to abundant wool and minimal grooming requirements.

German angora rabbits ("GAs" or "Germans") weigh in at 9 to 12 pounds. Among all the breeds, these rabbits will offer you the most fiber per bunny – and not just because of their size. They are famous for producing vast amounts of dense, lustrous, beautifully crimped fiber. (Well, perhaps not a *vast* amount of fiber in comparison to sheep or alpacas…) The average harvest of Germans is 10 to 16 oz. every 90 days! The breed was expressly developed for high production of easily harvested, maintenance-free fiber strong enough to handle milling. German rabbits do not "blow" (i.e. shed or molt) their coats, so require shearing. Shearing is not a difficult skill to learn. A good tutorial and a few rounds of practice will allow the novice owner to shear with confidence. Unlike the EAs, Frenchies and Satins, the German breed of angora rabbits is not currently recognized by the American Rabbit Breeders Association (ARBA). Instead, rabbits are registered through The International Association of German Angora Rabbit Breeders (IAGARB) group here in the USA. German angoras enjoy a reputation as the most easygoing and affectionate of the angora rabbits. GAs are perfect for situations where children will assist in handling the fiber pet(s).

The nitty gritty on Germans: the ultimate fiber producers! German angoras are the best choice for folks who want lots of wool, might get into the business of angora yarn and products and don't mind housing/ handling BIG rabbits.

Rosy, a German Angora doe from Katie Musante's rabbitry in Oregon. Sure, this photo may *look* small, but that rabbit is BIG!

On the other end of the spectrum from Germans, in terms of amount of fiber produced per rabbit, are the **Satin angoras ("Satins")**. Satins are famous for the impressive sheen, light weight and soft, silky hand of their coats. They are drop-dead gorgeous rabbits. Bunny owners swoon at the sight of them. Spinners twitch. Knitters have been known to actively drool while holding a skein of yarn spun from Satin wool. All this fibery excitement has its cost, though. Satins generally produce the least amount of wool per rabbit from amongst all the angora breeds. You will get slightly less wool per harvest than with Frenchies or EAs. The light weight and soft hand of their wool also means that

Satins have a tendency to matt easily. Breeders are working to offset this tendency, but you can still be assured that a Satin angora will require vigilant care and grooming. Keep the following formula in mind: high quality wool + high maintenance coat - limited harvest per rabbit = very expensive fiber. But for those willing to make the commitment, Satins can provide you with the highest quality fiber known for its there-is-nothing-like-it-in-this-world feel. The fiber community will thank you for your efforts. As for size, the Satins are in the middle range, matching the Frenchies at about 8-10 pounds each.

The nitty gritty on Satins: gorgeous rabbits with gorgeous fiber that requires attentive grooming.

Franco Rios shows off an armload of his beautiful Satin angoras.

The Nervous New Owner's Guide to **Angora Rabbits**

Giant angoras ("Giants") are considered a fifth, unique breed. They were developed by Louise Walsh, in the US, by crossing French Lops, Flemish Giants and German Angoras. Giants are still somewhat rare; their wool is not yet in wide use. But they are becoming increasingly popular! We are sure to see more of them -- and their fiber -- at festivals, shows and from fiber enthusiasts as time passes.

Crossbreeds and Others

A number of breeders are working to improve various aspects of angora rabbits by crossbreeding. Denoted by an X after the contributing breeds, these crosses make excellent fiber pets. If you are looking at crossbreeds as an option, be sure to ask the breeder questions about their stock. Most will enthusiastically discuss with you the selective breeding process, goals for their rabbitry and particular characteristics they are developing within their lines.

An **English/German X** has the lofty, soft coat of an EA along with the ease and bounteous fiber harvest of a German. It will also have reduced furnishings, which though amusing to view, contribute little to the harvest of usable fiber. English/German Xs may or may not molt, or "blow" their coats. Check with the breeder as to whether shearing is going to be required for that particular rabbit.

A very advantageous mix is a **Satin/French X**. Here, breeders are attempting to lighten the Satin's high maintenance requirements while maintaining the rich, silky coat for which it is famous. A clean head, feet and butt area are still present to keep grooming time down. The contribution of a heavier coat and higher percentage of guard hairs from the French breed helps reduce matting while maintaining the desired halo. It's a win/win situation for rabbit, owner and fiber enthusiast.

Another commonly seen hybrid is the **German/French X**. The addition of French to the German lines brings vivid color possibilities to an otherwise white rabbit. High percentage German hybrids carry the abundant fiber and body characteristics of the German lines, but have the color benefit as well.

It is worth mentioning that many folks own and spin wool gathered from **Jersey Woolies ("JWs").** These rabbits are not officially angoras. In fact, they are an entirely different breed of rabbit. However, they are so similar in appearance and have such strikingly similar coats to the angora rabbits that they deserve the rank of fiber pet. JWs have small, compact bodies and clean faces (i.e. no "furnishings"). Their fiber is somewhat shorter than that of most angora rabbits, but has sufficient length for spinning. Jersey Woolies are a wonderful, low maintenance option for first time fiber rabbit owners.

Agate, a blue chinchilla Jersey Wooley from Angora Moon Rabbitry in Deming, New Mexico.

The Nervous New Owner's Guide to **Angora Rabbits**

Colors

What makes color in the coats of rabbits? And why is the collectible fiber on angora rabbits usually so light in color? Color is the result of pigment contained within each hair on a rabbit's body. In fact, each hair has exactly the same amount of pigment, regardless of length. Therefore, the short hair found at face, ears and feet is the darkest. Longer hairs, especially the 3-4 inch long ones across the back and sides of the rabbit, look much lighter because the contained pigment is diluted over their length.

Without going into great detail, I'd like to provide you with a working vocabulary for color in angora rabbits. (And since this printing is in black and white, I recommend you go online and do an image search for any description that needs an accompanying visual!) Colors are assigned via detailed observations of fur, guard hair, color across areas of the body, color across the length of single hairs and skin color. For the novice owner, familiarity with the vocabulary of color will enable you to identify individual animals. Not to mention that it will make you feel like a pro!

One more helpful informational item regarding color... There are just three base colors found in angora rabbits: white, black and brown. The variety of shades, markings and patterns of the three colors is what gives the rabbit community its delightful and diverse vocabulary for color descriptions.

Single ("Self" or Solid) Color Rabbits

REWs (Red-Eyed Whites) are pure white rabbits with red eyes.

BEWs (Blue-Eyed Whites) are pure white rabbits with blue eyes.

Blacks have black or deep charcoal grey guard hairs, fur and skin.

Angoras not as deeply colored as Blacks are described as **Blues**. Their grey coloring is in the medium range and has a cool, bluish tint to it. Blues are the diluted form of black.

Chocolate bunnies are a lovely brownish-grey color. Their skin and guard hairs are deeply colored, while their fur tends to be lighter. The coats resemble a cup of coffee with lots of cream.

Lilac is the term used to denote bunnies with the very lightest shades of chocolate coloring. They also have a slight pinkish tint to their fur which can be described as "warm", as opposed to the "cool" tones of grey on a Blue rabbit. Lilac is the diluted form of chocolate.

Cream/Fawn/Red are all used as descriptions for rabbits whose coats are in the brown range with a reddish tint to the coat – from a very light, almost blonde (Cream), through a medium tawny-beige (Fawn), to the very deep rust-colored (Red).

Multiple Color Rabbits

Tortoiseshell ("Tort") bunnies have a range of colors that make their markings a delight to behold. Their face, ears, noses, feet and tail are of one color (usually dark) while their bodies have a single color across the top of their back that transitions to a different color on the sides and back of the bunny. The color of the face, ears, nose, feet and tail determine the name associated with the Tort (i.e. a dark brown face makes a chocolate tort, a blue-grey face makes a Blue Tort and so on).

Chinchilla ("Chin") rabbits have a complex coat, with the hair showing two bands of color separated by a definite break between each color. They can also have guard hairs in yet another, often darker, color dispersed throughout the coat. They can be more easily described as silver with black ticking.

Agouti are similar, but have three or more bands of color in the hair. They are various shades of brown with black ticking. This is the color pattern we see in wild rabbits.

Ticking is the description for dark guard hairs distributed through a rabbit's coat. It contributes to a rich, complex color across the rabbit's coat.

Pointed is the term used to describe a white rabbit with colored "points" on its ears, feet, nose and tail. For instance, a pure white rabbit with grayish ear tips, nose, etc., will be referred to as a Pointed Lilac.

Broken describes a primarily white rabbit with patches of any other angora coat color across its body. For instance, a white rabbit with patches of black is called a Broken Black.

The variety of colors and markings adds to the fun of owning angora rabbits and working with their fiber. What color range most appeals to you? Which coat would you like to see hopping around in your yard? Pick one or two -- or a few -- and enjoy the show.

A Note on Breeding

To breed or not to breed... that really IS the question. If you are new to angora ownership, I strongly recommend you delay breeding activity for at least a year. Two years? Even better.

Why do I want you to delay?

First of all, there will be plenty to learn about the care, feeding, grooming and harvest of fiber when you first become an angora rabbit owner. All that learning comes with its share of anxiety. Until you are comfortable with the tasks involved in rabbit care, you will be nervous and unsure of yourself. Having a litter of kits will increase that anxiety exponentially. Who needs that?

Secondly, a breeder of rabbits is expected to know a great deal. Breeders make themselves available to potential and ongoing customers for advice, demonstrations and information. If you are a new owner yourself, how realistic is it that you can assist others in this way?

Third, if you breed your rabbits before you know enough to assess their temperament, health and wool quality, you may be inadvertently contributing to the degradation of your angora breed.

Fourth, (and this is my own pet peeve, I'll admit) why create more angora rabbits when there are plenty out there that need a home? Angora rabbits are available through breeders, animal shelters, rescue organizations and from owners who need to rehome due to ill health, a move or some other life-altering circumstance. Before you make more rabbits, look around for bunnies in need and give them a home instead!

Having said all that... it does happen that one can have an "oops!" litter. It's especially common among new owners, as they aren't aware of just how sneaky rabbits can be when they want to (ahem!) reproduce. Be aware that rabbits can mate through a wire cage. Don't keep unaltered males and females in adjacent cages or accessible to each other during exercise. Spay and neuter as soon as possible.

If, however, your rabbits have spent time together while your guard was down, the first indicator that there might be a pregnancy is that your doe will begin pulling the wool from her butt area, legs, lower sides and tummy. She's doing this to gather wool for a nest. You'll also see her gather straw, timothy hay and any other appropriate materials in her mouth and carry them to her nesting site.

Note: A doe involved in these activities is not always pregnant. If she's spent time near a buck, even a neutered one, her hormones may prompt her to prepare for a pregnancy even though she's not actually pregnant. This is called a "false pregnancy". No need to worry, here. Just let her run around and build a nest. In a week or so, when she realizes she doesn't need it, she'll abandon it. You can take the gathered materials out of her cage or hutch at that time.

If there is a pregnancy, you will come upon the litter about 28-32 days after the rabbits have mated. Of course, if you were unaware of the mating in the first place, you're unlikely to know just when those kits might be due! But if you *do* happen to notice your doe acting as if she is pregnant, provide her with a wooden, plastic or cardboard box in her hutch or cage for a nesting site. It should have sides short enough to allow her to come and go while also being tall enough to prevent babies from falling out (4 to 8 inches will do).

Keep an eye out for the appearance of tiny, wriggling pink things in the nest she's building. The babies will be very small, with no fur on their bodies at all.

Tiny kits, just a few days old, at Chris Morgan's rabbitry.

Your doe will keep her kits warm and protected with the materials she's gathered for the nest. Even in very cold weather, a layer of her loose wool covering the kits will keep them warm. Check occasionally to make sure that newborns have not squirmed their way out from under the wool. You don't want their bodies to cool down too much until they've developed their own protective coat of downy fur.

Don't be too disappointed if your doe doesn't spend all her time in the presence of her kits. In the wild, rabbit mommies spend a lot of time away from their kits so as not to lead any predators their way. Your doe will only want to be with them when she is nursing. Be sure she can come and go at will. To assist kits in getting to the doe's milk without too much difficulty, trim the hair right around each of her nipples. Otherwise, there's not much you need to do. The strong instincts of the doe will direct her actions and those of her kits.

A cardboard box keeps kits in their nest while mom goes off to get some exercise. These kits are from an "oops!" litter when my adventurous English doe and sneaky Jersey Wooly buck met up.

If you find yourself with a surprise litter of kits, get connected to an online discussion. Folks there can answer all your questions and offer timely advice. You may want to locate a copy of *Completely Angora* by Sharon Kilfoyle and Leslie Samson. The book is now out of print, but is available used and remains the most complete published resource on angora rabbit care, including all aspects of breeding.

Life with Fiber Rabbit(s)

Ethel Ledger, accompanied by her
father, gives a smile while presenting
her angora rabbits. The photo was
taken at the mill in South Duffield,
Yorkshire (UK), circa 1920.

Housing

Preliminary Considerations

Compared to many other domestic animals, rabbits require minimal space and maintenance. They can be housed inside or outside, in a variety of structures, individually or as a group. Where you decide to keep them will depend as much on your lifestyle as on your rabbits' needs.

Information to consider:

• Angora rabbits are comfortable in a wide range of temperatures, especially on the cooler end of the spectrum. (Keep in mind their heavy wool coats!) Housing must **provide protection** from extreme heat (over 80 degrees F), extreme cold (below zero degrees F), wind, rain and predators.

• Rabbits create **urine and poop**. It's smelly, even if you clean their cages frequently. With that in mind, place your rabbit housing accordingly. One rabbit? Probably okay in the house. Two? Might want to move them into a largely unused room. Three or more? Start thinking about the garage or an outbuilding. Or, avoid the quandary altogether by providing your rabbits with outdoor housing. Many folks do -- including me. Keep in mind the olfactory impact on your neighbors. They will appreciate it.

• **Adequate space** around the cage or hutch is important. You will be cleaning things, moving large amounts of materials in and out of the area (shavings, timothy hay, drop pans, sections of cages, etc.). Leave yourself room to do what needs to be done.

• You will want **easy access to water**, both for filling water bottles and cleaning cages.

• Your rabbits will need **exercise**. Think about where they will do it, how you will get them there, how often they'll need to exercise and whether you will be required to supervise. You have a lot of options in this area, but start thinking about it right from the start.

Questions to consider:

• What makes the most sense for your situation – housing **inside or out**? In both settings, where will the rabbits be protected and safe?

• Do you want to **see and interact** with your rabbit(s) throughout your day or can they be somewhat removed from you? How much noise and activity will they be subject to?

• How will you **protect** the rabbit(s) from predators, curious strangers and careless visitors?

• If you are away from home, is your set up easy for someone to access, with necessary items near at hand for their **caretaking** role?

Bunnies and others...

Tyler Gould enjoys a snuggle with one of his family's angora kits.

Christine Durkin's EA Tank, and her cat, Spike, enjoy a snuggle as well!

Dogs and/or cats at your home? How about young children? Curious friends? If you let anyone or anything interact with your rabbits, **supervise, supervise, supervise!** Children can be rough in their handling of an animal without meaning to cause damage. They can also inadvertently allow a rabbit to escape, whether by dropping it or by leaving a door or gate open. Some dogs absolutely LOVE "their bunnies". But even the most mild-mannered of dogs has a predator instinct. Don't take any chances. Make sure all family members, friends, neighbors and even community utility workers (if you have outside housing and/or a bunny yard) know that **you must be present** for visits of any type.

Inside Housing

Let's say you have an extra bedroom that isn't in regular use. Or a garage that only houses "stuff" instead of a car. Perhaps you have a barn. Or a not-too-too-full-and-fairly-sturdy storage shed. Any of these settings would make a nice spot for your rabbit. All are considered "inside" housing. If one of these options is available, all you'll need to house your rabbit is a simple, wire cage. Hooray for you! Wire cages are easy to locate, inexpensive and easy to clean. You will find a wide variety of shapes and sizes available for purchase at pet supply stores, online rabbit specialty suppliers or at a general auction site like ebay.com. If you are handy, it's easy as pie to make one. Any general rabbit book or website will provide you with a list of required tools and supplies along with simple directions.

Spinner, one of my English REW does, sitting in a simple, homemade wire cage.

If you decide to purchase a wire cage, look for one that has a wire floor and an easily removable, metal or plastic litter pan. The pan should be located directly under the floor, with at least an inch between wire floor and the bottom of the pan. (I prefer a deep dropped floor -- with two or more inches of space available for litter. But that's just me.) Your rabbit's urine and poop, along with any debris in the cage, will fall right through to the pan below. Clean up is a snap. Simply slide out the litter pan (also affectionately known as the "poop pan"), dump, refill with fresh, clean litter and replace. You're done! Easy clean up means less procrastination. Less procrastination results in a healthier home for bunny and a nicer smelling environment for you both.

A closer view of the same cage. My homemade cage lifts from its metal pan to allow for cleaning. Most cages, however, are structured so that the cage remains stationary and the litter pan slides out.

The Nervous New Owner's Guide to **Angora Rabbits**

Some wire cages unhook from the drop pan on which they rest and are lifted off to allow for litter change and complete cleaning. Others are arranged such that the drop pan slides out from its resting place under the wire floor. Either arrangement works, as long as you are comfortable in handling it.

As for size, a commonly utilized wire cage for a single, medium-sized rabbit (8-10 lbs) is 30" x 36". If you have one of the larger breeds, you'll need something bigger. You may also choose to house bunnies together. Bonded pairs and siblings share especially well. Size accordingly!

One last option to consider: stacking cages. A number of animal cage and supply retailers offer a system whereby cages can be vertically stacked and secured. They look like bunny apartment buildings! I laughed when I first saw them. But once I thought about it, I realized what a boon they'd be to the space-challenged bunny owner. Such a clever idea!

There is ongoing discussion regarding whether wire cages are difficult for rabbits' feet. Breeders and owners disagree, with folks in the UK (a.k.a. England) promoting solid-floor cages as the more humane option. In this country, the majority of rabbits are housed in wire cages. It is worth noting that angora rabbits, unlike many other breeds, have feet thick with fur. The likelihood that they feel discomfort due to the wire seems remote. Nonetheless, some owners do provide a wooden, tile or padded surface in a cage as a "rest" for tender rabbit feet. Remember that any solid surface you put in the cage will soon be soiled. It's going to require frequent cleaning. In general, it's best to keep a watchful eye on the bunny feet in your care. Use "rests" if you feel they are needed and/or to ease your mind. But keep 'em clean. Check to make sure your wire floor has openings at least ½" x 1" wide that will support your rabbit's feet but still leave adequate space for droppings to fall through.

Outside Housing

No space inside your home for bunnies? Don't worry! Rabbits are perfectly comfortable living outdoors. Find a location with shelter from prevailing winds, shade in the summer and room for an adjacent exercise area. You're going to need more protection than a simple wire cage – a hutch is the right option for you.

A view of my "bunny yard". I have several commercially prefabricated wood hutches. In the summer, I keep the whole area covered with shade cloth.

Hutches are sturdy, wooden structures that provide a fully weatherized roof and closed sides. They are usually equipped with legs that lift the rabbit's living area above the ground. The wire front-panel allows you to hang equipment (water bottles, etc.) just as you would on a wire cage. Additionally, a solid or wire door makes up part of the front panel so you can take bunny in and out. Some hutch doors are vertically hinged. They open from the top and reach all the way to the ground, providing a ramp for bunnies to come and go. Look for a hutch with a hinged roof. It's much easier to snag bunnies from above than from reaching in through the front panels. A hinged roof makes cleaning a snap. Consider purchasing (or making) a hutch cover. Covers are often sold right alongside hutches. Made from waterproof fabric, they provide an additional layer of protection from especially harsh weather (rain, snow, howling winds, etc.). Check to be sure your cover allows light and air into the hutch.

Chris Morgan's French angora doe rests comfortably on the wire floor of her hutch.

Solid wood floors in hutches are common. They are especially favored in the UK. If you acquire a hutch with a solid floor, be sure you can access all parts of the interior for cleaning. Also, consider litter training your rabbits. Yes! Litter train them, just like a cat! Bunnies will pee and poop in the same area repeatedly.

Place a low-walled, plastic container or tray in their usual spot, filled with your choice of litter. A little timothy hay will encourage them as well. After they are used to using the litter tray, you'll be able to move it wherever you like. The bunnies will continue using it. Rather than having to clean every floor surface frequently, you can change out the litter pan frequently and then clean the rest of the hutch less frequently.

A great option for outside housing is what I call a "hybrid hutch". If you have the time and money to purchase, and/or the know-how to build, I highly recommend you look at this system for housing your rabbits. The "hybrid" hutch is a combination wire cage and wooden hutch. A wire cage with drop panel is fitted to easily sit inside a constructed wooden roof and wall structure. The wire cage remains removable from the structure, allowing you to use the cage for travel or to bring the rabbit inside for periods of time. Separating the two sections also increases your ability to effectively clean all parts of the cage. If you are building a hybrid hutch, you can make it to the exact size and shape you want, housing one wire cage or twenty!

If housing your rabbits outside, consider how you will deal with extremes of temperature – both in the height of summer and in deepest winter. There's a lot you can do to make your bunnies more comfortable. Remember, they will be fine out there. But as with people, a few added comforts can make a great difference.

Tips for Keeping Cool

- Even if you generally comb or pluck your rabbits to gather their wool, **shear** them for the summer. Shearing is especially important if you live where temperatures go higher than 85 degrees (F) and the humidity is high. Just like for humans, the less hair the better when it's hot out!

- Provide bunnies with **frozen water bottles!** Take disposable water bottles (from the single serving size to the one gallon jug size, depending upon your needs) and fill 3/4 full. Place in freezer until ready. Then distribute frozen bottles to cages, hutches and around the bunny yard. A similar technique is to keep ceramic tiles in the freezer until well cooled, then place in your bunny's cage or exercise area. Your rabbit will lie on the tile and give you a happy look!

Jolene Richardson keeps this square ceramic tile in her freezer until her bunny, Ruttiger, needs some summertime cooling down.

- Keep bunnies in **shade** as much as possible. If you don't have a porch or trees, consider putting up shade cloth over your bunny's home during the summer months.

- Introduce **evaporative cooling** by hosing down the ground near bunnies, the roof of your bunny barn, providing a mister or turning on a water sprinkler in their area occasionally.

- Use exhaust **fans** to move air around. Don't point the fans directly at your rabbit. Wind can be an irritant.

Tips for Keeping Warm

- **Keep an eye on drinking water** sources! Switch out water bottles frequently (at least twice per day, more often if your temperatures are very low) to insure your rabbits have access to unfrozen drinking water. Try to use larger water bottles, as they freeze less frequently than small ones. Make cozies for your water bottles! Knock out frozen water from dishes and replace often to insure access to drinking water.

- Drape an **old blanket** over the hutch, inside the roof, for an extra layer of insulation. Provide straw or extra timothy hay for burrowing. If you haven't already, buy or make a **hutch cover.**

My Jersey Wooly buck checks out the snow from his blanket-covered hutch in the "bunny yard".

The Nervous New Owner's Guide to **Angora Rabbits**

- In extremely cold climates, consider using **metal or hard rubber water dishes** during the winter. Plastic bottles and dishes will occasionally crack when frozen. Metal is far more resilient. To replace frozen water, dip the metal dish in a bucket of hot water and pop the ice block out.

- Check out the option of using **heated water bottles**. They are not prohibitively expensive and can be found online and at area feed stores.

- **Heat lamps** are a great option for mitigating cold temperatures. Remember to keep the cord inaccessible to the rabbit's cage and exercise areas! Look for the red bulbs, commonly used for warming newborn chicks, which provide wonderful warmth without too much light.

Accessory Equipment

Along with the cage or hutch, you'll need a few items to make your bunny happy and healthy in its new home. Be sure to have these on hand:

- **Water bottle(s)**. I recommend purchasing the largest available – otherwise you will be refilling it every ten minutes. Believe me... that gets old very quickly. Water bottles should be cleaned occasionally with a little bleach to prevent build up of algae. It's best to have two on hand for every cage or hutch you own. That way, you always have a spare bottle to provide your rabbit while the other is being cleaned.

- **Food dish/pellet hopper.** Purchase a dish which hangs suspended from the wires of your cage or hutch. Use wire or trash bag ties to secure it in place. (Bunnies love to nudge the dishes up and down, dislodging them, spilling the contents and then kicking around their amusing new toy.) A small, ceramic crock will also work as a dish. Make sure it's weighty!

- **Toys.** Stuck in a cage most of the time? Your rabbit could use some distractions. Try throwing in a whiffle ball or a toilet paper roll stuffed with timothy hay. Hard plastic children's toys and teething rings are wonderful because they are designed to make noise, move around easily and are hard enough that the rabbit can gnaw on them without ingesting any plastic. Some bunnies love to mess around with an old towel. Most anything works! Novelty is the key with toys; introduce something new every few weeks or occasionally switch out the toys you have on hand.

Susan Helgeson's buck, Zorro, gives a mischevious glance before entering his cardboard tube.

- **Extra wire** or trash bag twist ties. I use these constantly to secure equipment in place or annoy my rabbits by suspending toys from their exercise area.

- **Lidded plastic bins and/or garbage cans.** Useful for keeping food, cleaning supplies, shaving/litter and other items close at hand. Also helpful in keeping out curious critters and protecting contents from the elements.

The Nervous New Owner's Guide to **Angora Rabbits**

- **Exercise area.** Provide bunnies with a safe place to exercise by either fully enclosing a section of yard for their use, setting up temporary play areas with wire or plastic pens (called "exercise pens", fully collapsible and marketed to dog owners) or let them run around your kitchen, garage or house. If they are not in an enclosure, keep an eye on them for safety reasons. And... remember that bunnies dig! Any area used consistently by the rabbits will need a solid floor or buried chicken wire to keep your friends from tunneling right out of your yard.

Ruttiger, an English angora, sprints over to get treats from his owner, Jolene Richardson. "Did you say parsley?!?!?"

Keeping It Clean and Healthy

Inside or outside, the housing you've provided must be kept clean and sanitary for the sake of your rabbit's health. Change litter pans often. Build up of feces and urine is not only unpleasant to humans, it creates ammonia, an irritant to bunny breathing.

Changing bunny litter pans is like scooping cat litter or picking up the backyard if you have dogs – a necessary, though unpleasant chore which is part of life with animals. The longer you delay, the more unpleasant the chore becomes. So don't procrastinate. A small whisk broom or scrub brush is nice to have on hand; use it to brush litter out of corners and off ledges.

Periodically, you must thoroughly **clean and disinfect** your rabbits' housing. Washing with soap isn't enough. You've got to disinfect as well, to prevent development and transmission of disease. I call this two-part process "the complete scrub down". The frequency with which you "scrub down" depends entirely upon the number of rabbits you have per cage/hutch, your tolerance for filth, your energy level/available time and the maintained health of your rabbits. Truly fastidious owners scrub down their cages monthly. Some only take on the task once per year, with intermittent spot cleaning as needed.

You can use any mild soap for the cleaning part. I use dishwashing liquid or liquid castile soap (like Dr. Bronner's). For disinfecting, it's best to obtain a solution that is non-toxic and made specifically for use with animals. You can find safe disinfectants at feed stores, animal specialty stores or online from rabbit suppliers. If you have one, you can also use a propane torch on your wire cages to clean and sterilize.

Since my hutches are located outside and predominantly house single rabbits in each, I do the scrub down twice per year. I choose a weekend day in the fall or spring. I make sure that the weather is nice, I have no other responsibilities and that I have on clothes appropriate for getting wet and filthy. Then I roll up my sleeves and get started. Here's my process for the complete scrub down:

- First, I remove all the rabbits from their hutches and the bunny yard. I set them up in a completely separate area. I don't want to have to worry about them underfoot or escaping into the rest of the yard (though the dogs would love it!)

• I pull all water bottles, trays and attachments of any kind from the hutches (or cages) and set them aside for individual cleaning. Litter pans are removed. So are all removable wire floors. I take pans and wire floors and soak them in a big plastic tub full of soapy water. I then scrub them with a brush or green scrubby , make sure I've gotten every side of each piece, rinse with hose, then set in the sun to dry.

• Next I take the hose over to my hutches and rinse each one with water, scrub out with brush and soapy water, then rinse with hose again. Here's where the non-toxic soap is important, as my rabbits will return to their yard while soapy water is still present. This way I make sure it won't harm them.

• When litter pans and wire floor sections are dry, I spray them down with a disinfectant (I use Vanodin, diluted to the advised level in a plastic spray bottle) and set them back in the sun. While they are drying, I spray all interior surfaces of the hutch with the same disinfectant.

• At this point, I usually address all the small equipment. Water bottles get soaked in the kitchen sink in a very diluted bleach solution then rinsed thoroughly. Food and hay trays get scrubbed down and sprayed with disinfectant just like the larger equipment.

• Once everything is dry, I return all parts to the hutch, fill with fresh shavings, re-attach water bottles and food trays and let the bunnies back in!

Of course, you will vary your process for the scrub down based upon the type and location of your housing. But the process, in some form, does need to be done on a regular basis. It's a big job. I won't downplay the time or effort involved. But it does give me a good feeling to know the hutches are clean and that I am providing a safe, healthy home for my rabbits. That peace of mind is worth any amount of elbow grease!

Temporary Housing and Transport

Don't forget that you will need some kind of carrier for your rabbit. A carrier will come in handy at initial purchase/pick up, trips to the vet and journeys beyond your home (i.e. taking bunny to your child's show and tell). Provide your rabbit with a space not much larger than he is, with access to water and plenty of air. A rabbit will be more comfortable if there is not much noise or movement during transport. For long distances, you will want to provide hay and a few pellets. Don't be surprised if your rabbit doesn't eat. Rabbits rarely eat when they are nervous. Special transport cages are available through any cage supplier. But cat (and small dog) carriers work just as well and are less expensive.

Plastic "cat carriers" work quite well for short trips and are easy to disassemble for cleaning.

Feeding

In direct opposition to children, guests and friends with special diets, your rabbits require almost no effort to feed and water. Here's all you need to provide:

• **Clean, accessible water.** Use a small-animal, gravity fed water bottle attached to your cage or hutch. The type with a ball on the end are easiest for bunnies to figure out. Bowls or crocks can be used in a pinch, but avoid long term use as the bunnies love to move them around, spilling the water. In addition, rabbits tend to develop matts around the face and neck due to faces dipped in bowls.

• **Good quality, fresh pellets.** To find the appropriate feeding amount, give your rabbit ½ cup of pellets per day and increase the amount slowly until you begin to see pellets still in the dish at the next feeding time. Then back off just a bit on the amount you feed. You are there! Most angoras will eat between a ½ cup and a full cup of pellets per day (English on the lower end, and Germans/Giants on the upper end). Growing kits will eat ravenously, so don't be surprised if you put out copious amounts of pellets while they grow to their adult size. Feed pellets once per day or split amount equally and feed twice per day, as your schedule allows.

• **Timothy hay.** Something to keep in mind about hay for rabbits is that you want to provide a grass hay (like timothy or orchard grass) rather than a legume hay (like alfalfa). Legume hay is much too high in protein and calcium. Bunnies can "free feed" on hay, meaning you keep a supply always available to them. They will not overeat and you will not have to worry about hunger if pellets get delivered a little later than usual.

• Additional items for consideration:

  - High protein **pellet supplement** (like Calf Manna, Starshine, or Showbloom) given as treats or mixed into their regular pellets at 10-20%. You can also look for YQ+, a supplement on the market made by King Feed, which is excellent for gut health, getting reluctant animals to eat, and helps reduce ammonia smells in your barn.

  - **Herbs or greens** that provide beneficial nutrients include dandelion, raspberry/blackberry/strawberry leaves, comfrey, borage, parsley, plantain, sage, oregano, lemon balm, and the leaves and small twigs of willow and fruit trees (but not the stone fruit trees such as peach, plum, etc.). Beware of poisonous plants (i.e. tansy, foxglove, rhubarb, etc.) If you are unsure of the plant, don't give it to your rabbits!

  - **Fruits and vegetables**. One big chunk per day is a quite welcome treat for a rabbit. Beware of feeding too many fruits or carrots, as rabbits don't need much sugar. Try out different vegetables to see what's popular. My rabbits swoon over arugula and tiny bits of broccoli!

- **Papaya tablets** help your rabbit pass accumulated wool in their stomach. Try to find tablets that are free from sugars and fillers. One to three tablets a week is usually sufficient. After shearings, after does pull wool for their nests and when rabbits are blowing their coats are times when these tablets can be very beneficial. You can also feed fresh or dried **pineapple and papaya bits**. Look for the kind without added sugar. I give my rabbits two tiny chunks of dried papaya daily, as a reward for hopping up into their hutches at night. I also give tiny bits as I'm grooming and harvesting, to positively reinforce good behavior.

Deb Boyken snapped this picture of her friend Jessica's angora rabbit mid-bite. Another second's hesitation and that parsley would have been GONE!

Handling

Bunnies do not like to be high up off the ground. It's not natural for them. They panic, struggle and generally put up a big fuss. Help your rabbit feel safe. Learn to pick it up and hold it securely. Any of these methods work for you.

• **The "football" hold:** Picture a football player running for the end zone, the ball tucked safely under his arm. Now replace that football with a bunny and you've got the idea! To get your rabbit from cage or table to football position, place one hand under the rabbit's chest and the other on top of it's rump area. Lift the rabbit, using both hands, and tuck it, head first, into the crook of one arm. Hold firmly against your body. You are holding the rabbit in place by the use of your arm, the side of your body and your hand on its rump. Once secured, you can release your hold on its rump -- leaving you with one free hand.

Sophie, my blue French X doe, in a football hold.

Well, THERE'S the fluffball's head! (We were wondering...)

The Nervous New Owner's Guide to **Angora Rabbits**

- **The "baby" hold:** Most folks will inadvertently use this hold on their first handling of a rabbit. It works fine on some rabbits, but isn't as successful with willful rabbits who don't want to be picked up. The mistake made is in not supporting the feet while transferring the rabbit from cage to chest. Be sure to have a hand securely on the rabbit's rump for support and one on or under its chest. Then lift the rabbit to rest against your chest, with the length of one arm supporting its body securely against you. The rabbit can face you, head up toward yours and body parallel with yours – or can also be comfortable slung to the side, again with the length of one arm securing the rabbit's body against your own.

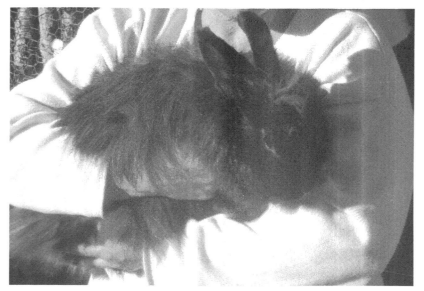

Zia, the herd "queen", prefers to be carried in the baby hold.

- **The "rag doll":** Occasionally, a rabbit will be most comfortably carried in what looks like a careless hold. After lifting the rabbit (as previously described), turn it to face away from you and secure with one arm across its chest, under the arms. Hold the rabbit firmly against your body. It's legs will hang down and it will resemble a floppy rag doll in the arms of child. It's not the most common hold, but when others fail, this is often the one that provides comfort and security to a rabbit.

Christine Durkin, with her blue English doe, Olivia, showing us the ragdoll hold.

When you've arrived at your destination, give your bunny a feet-first landing, whether facing away or toward you. The rabbit will feel secure right away and won't struggle to jump the last few feet to the ground or table. Once landed, a rabbit will likely begin exploring unless you place a hand on it to keep it in place. Use gentle pressure on its head, neck or back to let it know you want it to stay put. Long, heavy strokes across the head, ears and body will help calm the rabbit.

I keep one hand on my French buck Cap'n Jack, while grooming him with a rake. My hutches happen to be a perfect height to serve as a work surface!

When the rabbit seems relaxed into his new surroundings, you can begin grooming or checking his health. When finished, resume petting for a bit to reinforce a pleasurable experience with your handling of the rabbit. Pick up in one of the described manners and return to hutch or cage. Remember, provide a feet-first landing for the rabbit. Or, if applicable, simply place the rabbit on the ground and let him approach and enter his cage in his own time. Providing a treat in the cage each time you return the rabbit will help motivate/train him that returning to his cage results in a good thing!

Grooming

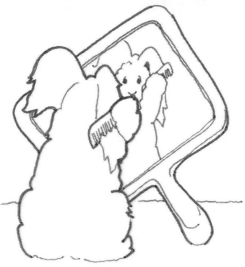

Angora rabbits, much like sheep, were bred over hundreds of years to develop a coat of wool for humans to harvest. And like sheep, angoras are dependent upon us for the cyclical grooming and removal of that coat in order to remain healthy. Aside from the regular harvesting of the wool coat, you will need to groom the rabbit frequently. Set aside a regular time for this activity. It's best to have ample time so the pace of working with your rabbits is relaxed. Some grooming sessions will be simple, with very little to take care of. Others will be more involved, especially if you identify problems that need additional care and attention.

Brushing Out Your Bunny

Depending upon the breed and particular coat of your rabbit, you will need to groom anywhere from once per week to once a month. English angoras generally need brushing every week. Most German angoras don't require any between-shearing brushings. They only require a mid-point clipping job of the vent area and behind the ears. Take each rabbit individually out of their cage. Check them visually to make sure all is well with coat, eyes, feet, area around neck and between ears and anus/ reproductive organs. Then, with grooming tool of your choice, brush through the rabbit's coat, removing loose hair and debris. If the rabbit is not molting, or "blowing" his coat, there will not be a great deal of hair to gather. Use a bristle brush, steel comb, a "rake" or any other type of grooming tool which feels comfortable in your hands and does the job. As a rabbit's coat goes through its cycle of growing, thickening and then shedding (while starting a new coat's growth underneath), you may find yourself switching tools. It's not unusual for an owner to keep half a dozen different types of grooming tools on hand, especially if there are different breeds of rabbits in the herd.

Items in my grooming tool basket: papaya bits and parsley for treats, a small pair of sharp scissors, two steel combs, grooming rake and a small steel brush.

Life with **Fiber Rabbit(s)**

Mats

Most grooming is actually about searching for and getting rid of mats in a rabbit's coat. Mats result from moisture and friction. Hair becomes tangled back onto itself and forms a dense clump of fur. If left unresolved, the mat will grow in size and become uncomfortable and unhealthy for the rabbit. Mats can be found anywhere on the body, but most often develop on feet, rump, neck and face area. When you find a mat, don't panic! All rabbits get them from time to time. They are not the mark of a delinquent owner! Cast aside those guilty feelings and settle yourself to the task of getting rid of the mat as soon as you find it. Try any of these techniques:

- **Cutting:** The simplest way to remove a mat from a rabbit is to simply cut it off. Use your fingers to locate and identify its full outline. If there is sufficient room, maneuver a small pair of scissors in place between the mat and the rabbit's body. Ready a small section of rabbit hair as if to cut it, then deliberately rotate the scissors away from the rabbit's skin at a 45 degree angle. This rotation moves the cutting edges away from the rabbit, insuring you will not nip the skin. Clip that section of hair, then ready a new section, rotating your scissors prior to cutting once again. Repeat, cutting small sections of hair, until you have released the mat from the rabbit's coat. Pull the mat free. Check to remove any additional loose hair in the immediate area. Run a brush or steel comb over the area to be sure the entire mat has been removed.

- **Brushing out:** If you are uncomfortable with the idea of approach your bunny with scissors just yet, try brushing out the mat. Since it is composed of tangled hairs, a slow, consistent and ever deeper brushing might detangle the entire snare. Use a small, steel bristled brush (usually called a "spot groomer" or "mat buster"). Place your hand between the rabbit's skin and the mat itself, to help mitigate the tugging you are about to inflict on your rabbit. Gently begin brushing the mat's surface to detangle the top layer of hair. As they separate, apply more pressure and work your way slowly through the layers of the mat. Brushing out a mat takes time and patience. It is not very pleasant for your rabbit. But it does mean you will have an intact coat to harvest. If you check the rabbit frequently, you will identify mats before they become too large to brush out.

• **Breaking up:** If the mat is in a difficult location or is very large, a good way to approach it is to break it into smaller pieces before cutting or brushing it out. Use scissors to cut off the majority of the clump, then work out the remaining portion by brushing or pulling the hair free. You can also make multiple, parallel cuts into a large mat. These cuts will help you get at the root of the mat for easier removal. Apply cornstarch. Sprinkle some on the mat, both top and bottom and on the surrounding hair. Cornstarch is non-toxic and acts as a lubricant. It will assist the hairs in loosening from each other. When finished with your ministrations, simply pat the rabbit's coat to dislodge the white powder. Take time to work through your rabbit's entire coat, taking care to address furnishings if relevant. The areas around chin, cheeks and ears are easy to keep mat free if you comb or brush them regularly. Prevention is the best approach, as rabbits do not appreciate your coming at them with a pair of scissors aimed at their eyes, nose, mouth or ears. It's better to brush to prevent mats than to have to remove them once they've developed.

Hard to Reach Places

One of the most challenging aspects of grooming is getting to those hard to reach spots: tummy, legs and butt area. Here are a few ways to position your rabbit so you can reach everywhere that needs attention!

Bunny on its side:

While grooming, help your rabbit turn onto its side by gently adjusting its body into place. Most rabbits lie this way when they are relaxed, so if yours is hesitant, pet it for a while and give nose rubs until it calms. Groom what you can reach, then switch bunny to the opposite side to finish.

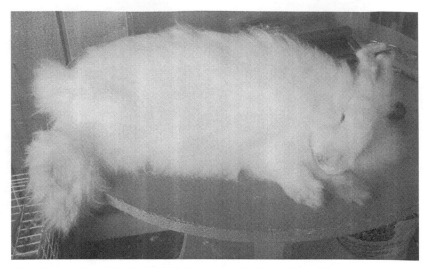

Christine Durkin's REW German X doe, Sigrid, gets ready for a bit of belly brushing.

Bunny on its back:

Some rabbits are completely fine with spending time in this position. Others hate it and will struggle violently. If you can, take some time to get your rabbit used to being held this way long before you have to spend time grooming it. Have a breeder show you the best way to turn a rabbit onto its back or do a search on youtube.com -- there are several sample videos which will show you the technique. Practice frequently. Always give your rabbit a treat when you are finished, to leave them with a positive impression of the experience. Keep inverted grooming sessions short at first (10-15 minutes), then gradually lengthen. If you have a second person to help, you can cradle the rabbit in your arms like a baby. Your assistant can then groom and trim as needed. If you are alone, set the rabbit on your lap and hold its head firmly with your knees, body parallel to your legs. Keeping its ears and head secured by your knees will allow you to use both hands for grooming work.

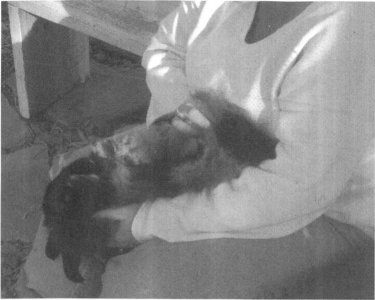

Zia shows off her "bunny on its back" technique! When I need to use my hands, I simply hold her head and ears between my knees.

Nail Clipping

You may want to clip your rabbits' toenails. Clipping prevents nails from becoming so long that they break – causing pain and bleeding for the rabbit. Use a small set of clippers, sized for a rabbit or cat. It is helpful to have good light in which to work. If you hold up the nail with the light behind it, the quick is easily visible. Clip the nail just in front of the quick, where it starts to curve. If you happen to nip the quick and get bleeding, place the nail in styptic powder, cayenne or cornstarch. Regular access to an exercise area with concrete, stone or gravel surfaces will help to wear down those pointy nail ends.

Behaviors

If you are at all like me, you'll get a real kick out of watching your rabbits. They have such personality! I love to start my days by pouring a cup of coffee and heading out to the rabbit yard. There I sit, sipping, waking up, watching, and chuckling from time to time – completely entertained by their antics. They run and romp, interact and then resolutely ignore each other (and me). I also enjoy my time with individual rabbits – usually while grooming or harvesting wool. Some are very interactive, others less so. But in general, angora rabbits are quite communicative, if you know how to read bunny language.

Grooming
Behavior: rabbit licking another rabbit with consistent, long strokes of tongue; sometimes a bit of chewing goes on as well.

(Bunny language) translation: "I'm okay, you're okay. Let's hang out."

Chinning
Behavior: rabbit rubbing his/her chin up against inanimate objects like cages, chairs, pieces of wood, rocks, shoes, crocks, etc.

Translation: "Mine! Mine! Mine! I like this! Mine!"

Stomping
Behavior: rabbit, while attempting to evade your grasp or having just escaped it will stomp one or two back feet loudly and sometimes make a growl or grunting noise.

Translation: "I do NOT like that. Not even a little bit. And I'm very annoyed with you, by the way."

Alternate Translation: "Please don't eat me! I'm just a little bunny. Why does everything like to eat us?!?!?!"

Burrowing/Digging
Behavior: rabbit fidgets and then starts digging furiously with front paws.

Translation: "I'm so OVER this whatever-it-is that you think we need to be doing. Let's get on to the next thing. NEXT!!!"

Bunny Flop aka "Chill Bunny"
Behavior: rabbit lying on side, head up, feet poking out from under body, or lying on stomach with front feet forward and back feet stretched out behind.

Translation: "I am relaxed. All is right with the world. The only thing that could possibly make me happier is a piece of papaya."

Mounting and/or Fighting
Behavior: rabbit chase, mount (i.e. humping, regardless of either rabbit's gender), bite or wrestle with another rabbit to establish which is dominant

Translation: "I am TOO the boss of you!"

Periscoping
Behavior: rabbit sits back on its rear legs and lifts its torso and front legs off the ground, head extended, sniffing around.

Translation: "Now THIS is worth investigating..."

Binkies
Behavior: rabbit jumps into the air, twisting head and tail in opposite directions; can be done from a standing position or whilst running about in a frenzy.

Translation: "Hee hee! Ha ha! Ho ho! Yippee!!! Wahoo! Yo, dude -- Look at meeeeeeeee!!!!!"

Health Notes

CAUTION! New owners of angora rabbits are likely to react to the first possible signs of sickness in their rabbits with wild anxiety, a profusion of worried emails, frantic calls to friends, breeders and county extension agents and a sudden willingness to drive 800 miles to the nearest rabbit specialist. If you or anyone you know exhibits these symptoms of New Owner Anxiety Disorder, quickly administer a cup of hot tea, murmur reassuring sentiments and sit back to wait it out. Once the rabbit has been diagnosed and the medicine administered, all will be well again (indeed as calm as it was prior to the sickness). Individuals with NOAD also exhibit severe memory loss and are often heard to murmur (well after the episode) "Oh c'mon now... I was never that worried. Surely you exaggerate!"

The best defense against sickness in rabbits is an attentive, prevention-oriented owner. Purchase healthy rabbits. Provide appropriate hydration and nutrition. Keep the rabbits and their living areas clean. Check your rabbits frequently for their level of activity, body condition and feeding/drinking. If you start with healthy rabbits and take good care of them, it's unlikely they'll contract any serious disease.

But rabbits, like all animals (including humans!), get sick from time to time. It's unavoidable. Common maladies among animals are exactly that – common. A sick rabbit is not a reflection of your capability as an owner! I've yet to meet or even hear of an owner or breeder that hasn't dealt with a sick rabbit at one time or another. It comes with the territory. So when it happens, don't feel guilty. I give you permission to feel worried and anxious, to wring your hands, pull out some hair, pace back and forth – whatever helps. There is nothing worse than caring for a tiny being with whom you cannot communicate. It's just terrible. But most of the time, it's not going to be a serious matter. You can prepare yourself for this eventuality by taking the following steps before any of your rabbits get sick:

• **Get connected with an online discussion/information group and/or a local group of rabbit fanciers.** I cannot stress the importance of this resource enough. They are your first line of defense against all possible troubles that might arise with your rabbits. See a symptom? Post it online and ask what the heck it could be. You'll quickly hear back and receive both knowledgeable responses and excellent advice on next steps. Ditto if there is a local angora rabbit community or nearby, reputable breeder. Anyone involved with angora rabbits will be happy to help you troubleshoot. That's just the way rabbity folks are.

• **Locate a vet who specializes in rabbits** (often referred to as a specialization in "exotic" animals). The likelihood that you will need to access a vet is small. But it's still worth a great deal to know who is out there in your community. Identify the nearest rabbit vet as soon as you become an owner. Alert him/her to the fact that you live in the community, have angora rabbits, are interested in whether they have experience with this particular kind of rabbit and that you're likely to call on them if anything serious develops regarding the health of your rabbits. Having a ten minute conversation with an appropriate vet will give you great peace of mind.

• **Download, bookmark or purchase a good resource on rabbit diseases.** Nothing eases the worried mind of an angora owner like clutching a big, fat book full of detailed information (except, of course, the first two steps listed above). Online or in the real world, get right to it and read, read, read. You will gain valuable information. You will be distracted from worrying. Both are helpful when you've got a sick rabbit on your hands.

Listed below are the health problems most common to angora rabbits. The majority of them are not serious, though some can develop into life-threatening issues. Once you've identified a problem, treat immediately. Have treatments on hand and ready for administering. At the very least, know where the can be obtained quickly. Why the urgency? As prey animals, rabbits have become highly skilled at hiding illness. By the time you notice something is wrong, your rabbit is likely in need of immediate treatment. Again, attentive, preventative care is the key to maintaining your rabbit's health.

Digestive Difficulties

Clean water, good food and plenty of exercise go a long way toward keeping an angora rabbit's digestive track in a state of health. So does this: from the moment you bring home your first rabbit, consider yourself on permanent "poop patrol". Check the state of your rabbit's feces whenever you have a chance. You want to see firm, round poops about the size of a pea (larger from large breeds). You may also see night feces, which is excrement that looks a bit different, and often the rabbits will go back and ingest these. Normal poop means all is well with your bunny. And with angora rabbits, the biggest threat to their digestive health is wool block. It can be fatal. Wool block occurs when the rabbit ingests so much hair that its body cannot expel the mass. Their digestive system becomes completely blocked and they eventually perish. It doesn't happen often, but it is a danger for this breed – so be on patrol. Checking poop will also give you a "heads up" when your rabbit is experiencing stress or has eaten something which is causing ill health. Also monitor your rabbit's intake of food and water. Any changes, especially a rabbit who has stopped eating and drinking completely, is also an indicator that something is wrong.

You See: round poops connected by strands of hair (commonly called "pearl necklace" or "necklacing")

It Could Be: your rabbit is ingesting a great deal of wool and you must pre-empt any possibility of wool block

To Treat: switch rabbit to water and hay only (no pellets) for a few days; provide a digestive aid like papaya tablets, dried papaya, fresh pineapple or its juice, or dandelion greens; get the bunny moving/exercising; resolve to incorporate a preventative regiment of administering digestive aids on a regular basis for several months. My bunnies get one to two chunks of dried papaya every day. They love it! I also give them tiny pieces as I'm grooming to both reinforce that handling results in something good and to offset the wool I know they will ingest as they groom after my handling them.

or...

You See: diahrrea and a "messy butt"

It Could Be: something is very wrong in your rabbit's system, though it could be the result of a few different things (stress, eating something which did not agree with the tummy, extreme temperatures, etc.)

To Treat: switch rabbit to water and hay only (no pellets) for a few days; provide a digestive aid like papaya tablets, dried papaya, fresh pineapple or its juice, comfrey or dandelion greens; get the bunny moving/exercising; resolve to incorporate a preventative regiment of administering digestive aids on a regular basis for several months. Willow branches and leaves are good for upset stomach; raw oats are beneficial for firming up stools. To keep the mess to a minimum, clip the hair around your bunny's bum.

or...

You See: rabbit is not eating and/or drinking

It Could Be: again, something is wrong with the health of the rabbit and this is a symptom – could be sluggish gut or any of the above maladies

To Treat: Induce exercise; tempt your rabbit with a few fresh foods (like parsley or fresh grass) or grains (whole oats or barley); make sure there is timothy hay available at all times as when the rabbit does decide to eat, it will be the best food to help; provide Pedialyte if rabbit is in danger of becoming dehydrated.

Respiratory Difficulties

Occasionally rabbits exhibit difficulties breathing. Respiratory maladies may be in response to environment or caused by a viral infection.

You See: occasional sneezing or coughing

Which Could Be: common allergies, a response to a litter pan that needs to be changed or something caught in the rabbit's nose, mouth or eyes

To Treat: change litter pan immediately and do so more frequently than you have before; check cage/hutch to be sure there is adequate air circulation; try changing type of bedding; check rabbit visually and with hands to make sure there is nothing lodged in or near eyes, nose or mouth; carefully monitor to determine which changes (introduced one at a time) make a difference in the frequency of symptoms. Good ventilation, clean cages, quality food (low on fine particles) and hay (free of dust, mold or any other contaminants) go a long way toward providing protection from respiratory difficulties.

or...

You See: rabbit sneezing or coughing and a wet, runny nose with white discharge, sticky matting on inside of rabbit's front legs due to frequent rubbing/wiping nose, a visibly tilted head

Which Could Be: a cold or snuffles (also called "pasteurella") – a highly contagious, viral infection which resembles the human cold and sometimes doesn't get cured, only reduced to periods of chronic activity

To Treat: isolate rabbit from the rest of the herd; administer appropriate dosages of Ivomec (per weight of rabbit, oral or shot available through animal feed and supply stores); clean and sterilize all cages/hutches immediately; look at introducing a preventative maintenance dose of Ivomec on a regular basis to protect your rabbits from further progression; consider culling any rabbit with a chronic infection in order to protect a larger herd. There is now scientific evidence that pasteurella can only get a hold of your rabbit's system if ammonia is also present in their environment. Control ammonia by keeping trays and cages clean and introducing a supplement (i.e. Showbloom or YQ+) to keep ammonia levels low in your rabbit's urine.

Wounds/Irritation

You See: a cut, scrape or gash on your bunny

Which Could Be: the result of fighting, an accident or a grooming nip (which happens from time to time, so don't be too freaked out!)

To Treat: clean the wound with a disinfectant (hydrogen peroxide or soap and water), apply protective salve or antibiotic ointment to wound (but hold bunny and pet bunny for a period of time to prevent him/her from directly licking it off), check frequently for status of wound and repeat cleaning/disinfecting until you see the wound begin to heal. You might also trim back the fur in the area directly around the wound, to prevent the hairs from getting into it and irritating it. Use a sharp pair of scissors and trim carefully as close to the skin as possible in an area about an inch wide around the wound.

or...

You See: "weepy" eyes, a discharge from eyes, noticeable tearing up and wet fur around eyes

Which Could Be: clear discharge indicates an irritant to the eyes, a colored discharge (usually a cloudy white, yellow or greenish tint) indicates some kind of bacterial infection

To Treat: using a warm wash cloth, gently moisten and clean the eye area to remove any discharge or dried, caked remains. Examine eye thoroughly to determine if there is anything lodged in the area – a likely culprit is a small piece of hay or a stray hair lodged somewhere between the eye and the top or bottom lid. Check to be sure there is nothing blowing air directly at the rabbits. If it's windy, provide a wind block or some kind of protection for your hutches. If you are using fans to cool your rabbit area, simply point them away from the cages. Once the irritant has been removed, the rabbits' eyes will slowly heal themselves. You can assist the process by applying a warm, wet washcloth periodically to moisten and remove discharge. If you are comfortable using medicinal herbs, moisten the washcloth in a hot tea made with goldenseal, comfrey or eyebright. If the eye issues are caused by something other than a foreign irritant, it may require veterinary assistance in order to heal.

Parasites

You see: dry, flaky skin in the fur across the back of the neck, butt area and sometimes also present in the side and back coat of the rabbit

Which could be: fur mites, a common malady among angora rabbits. Don't panic! This condition is easily treatable, doesn't bother the rabbits too much and the mites won't jump on you and become a problem in your household. Fur mites are mostly bothersome because they create a bunch of skin flakes that you DON'T want in your precious angora fiber! Unfortunately, fur mites are very contagious. If you've got them in one rabbit, you should go ahead and treat everyone.

To Treat: administer Ivermectin. It's a safe and effective medication to use on rabbits. Ivermectin (Ivomec Plus injectible 1% solution) is available at most feed stores or can be obtained from rabbit specialty stores over the internet. It's given orally or by injection, the dose determined by your rabbit's weight. Be aware that the dose for rabbits is very small! Consider using a diabetic insulin syringe to get an accurate measurement before administering. Injections are typically given subcutaneously at the skin over the shoulder area. Have a knowledgeable friend or a vet show you how. Once you've administered a dose, provide a follow-up dose 10-14 days later. Fur mites can be present in your rabbit's environment and will re-infect if not banished from the area, so be sure to thoroughly clean and disinfect your rabbit's home. You may want to give the area "the complete scrub down" every couple of weeks until you know the fur mites have been eradicated. Here's something to keep in mind: many angora owners administer a regular, preventative dose of Ivermectin to their rabbits. It's a safe and advantageous practice. Referred to as a "maintenance" dose, the regular administering of Ivermectin will protect your rabbits and insure a clean and healthy coat of wool.

or...

You see: irritation, scabbing and damage to the interior of the ears

Which Could Be: ear mites -- another fairly common malady

To Treat: administer Ivermectin, as described above

or...

You See: adult fleas on your bunny, yourself (during or after handling) or small, squirmy flea larvae, or ticks or lice or any other evil parasite that you know should not be present

Which Could Be: a transmittable parasite – fleas, lice or ticks.

To Treat: administer Ivermectin, Revolution or (kitty strength) Advantage. The one product you SHOULD NOT USE is Frontline – it is toxic for rabbits. If you have purchased a healthy rabbit and maintain a clean, healthy rabbit home, it's most likely that these evil adventurers have been introduced from somewhere else. Check any other animals you have (dogs, cats, etc.) and treat them for parasites as well. Be sure you do not have mice or other rodents moving through your outdoor rabbit area. Again, clean and disinfect cages and bunny exercise areas until all signs of the evil intruders are gone. Sigh with relief.

When to See the Vet

If you come across symptoms that are beyond what I've described here, or if the above maladies are not alleviated by the treatment described above, seek out a bunny vet. There may be an unusual or complex heath issue going on. Your bunny's health, as well as your peace of mind, will benefit from professional assessment and treatment.

As you're on the way to the vet's office, I recommend you have a serious, internal discussion with yourself about how much money you can reasonably spend on your rabbit. Modern veterinary science is a wonder -- and most everything can be treated, fixed, cured or remedied. But the bill for those services can be large.

Once the vet has examined your rabbit and has some assessment of the situation, clearly communicate with him/her the limits of your financial ability. Together, you and the vet can decide the best course of action. Don't feel guilty if you make the decision to put a rabbit down rather than spending the amount of money it requires for treatment. (Well, try not to.) Sometimes you have to accept that a rabbit is beyond your ability to help. It's not a good idea to financially imperil yourself in an effort to keep a sick or injured animal alive. The hundreds or thousands of dollars you don't spend at the vet that day will be needed to take care of the rest of your herd, a new bunny (or three), your family, your mortgage, your grocery bill, etc. And if you are able, try to keep anywhere from $200 to $500 tucked away somewhere for use in "bunny emergencies".

Losing a Rabbit

Rabbits die from old age, illness, accidents and neglect. It is an unavoidable aspect of owning, loving and working with rabbits. Their lifespan averages just 6 to 8 years. Sometimes you will not know *why* a rabbit has died. You will simply come out to visit and find the rabbit is still and quiet. Sometimes, a rabbit will pass away from old age. Sometimes it will be your decision to put him or her down, to spare further suffering in situations of injury or illness. Regardless of the manner of the death, it's always upsetting. If you do lose a rabbit, I suggest you

- Have a good cry.

- Bury your rabbit somewhere special. (I have a tradition of planting a new rose bush or flowering plant over each pet I've lost.)

- Pet your other bunnies, dogs, cats, chickens, mice, teenagers, spouse – whoever is around.

- Reflect upon the wonderful opportunity you had to enjoy your furry friend.

- Let your bunny-owning peers online know about your loss. They will offer great support and love, having been through it themselves a time or two.

Give yourself time to feel sad; know that your grief will lessen with the passage of time.

Working with Angora Wool

H..rv stin⍺ ⍺n-- St--r⍺⍺

Well now... you've picked up, brought home, housed, fed, watered, groomed, exercised and taken care of your rabbit. Here comes the reward! The very best part of owning an angora rabbit is harvesting and using the wonderful fiber. You will already have gathered some loose wool during grooming sessions. That's fine. Save it to add into the main harvest of wool. But you will gather a much larger amount of usable fiber during a harvest.

French, Satin, English and many of the X angora rabbits "blow their coat" (i.e. hairs loosen and are ready to come off the bunny) just about every three months. In other words, they shed. Yes, just like dogs and cats. Only this hair is useful! And you won't be using a vacuum cleaner to gather it up. If you take a close look at your bunny, you'll see tufts of hair which you can easily grasp and pull right off. Part your bunny's locks and look at the base of the hair, near the skin – can you see new, shorter hair there? That's your rabbit's new coat coming in. So you needn't worry that your bunny will be bald after harvest.

Angora owners harvest wool in two ways: plucking and shearing. **Plucking** is accomplished by working over the rabbit's entire body with your hands and/or a comb, gently pulling out or "plucking" the loose hair. **Shearing** indicates that you remove the entire coat by cutting it off. For owners of German angoras (and some

German crosses), your only option is to shear, as your rabbit's coat doesn't molt. Shearing does tend to go more quickly than plucking, and is often a good idea for folks with many rabbits. Plucking can be quite a lot of intricate work with your hands. If you choose to harvest by plucking, try doing it in multiple sessions to keep your muscles from getting sore and to keep your bunny from getting antsy. A lot of petting and treats will help!

General Directions for Plucking

• Work with your bunny on your lap, a table or grooming stand – whichever feels most comfortable to you. Always keep one hand gently placed on your rabbit so it knows you want it to stay put.

• Administer a preliminary "comb through" with a steel comb or grooming rake. You'll be separating and loosening the hairs, which helps the plucking go much faster.

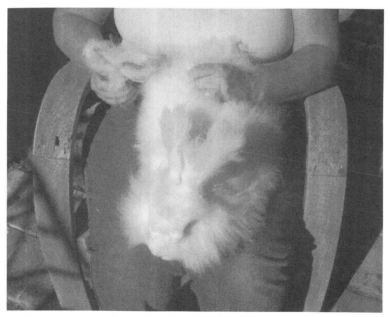

Spinner, one of my English REW does, gets her preliminary "comb through".

Observe which parts of the body release hair easily (by noting the amount of fiber gathered in your comb or rake). Many rabbits blow their coats in sections, over a few days. Some areas may not be ready for harvesting. You'll become aware of where to start plucking during the comb through.

• Starting with the area that is releasing the most hair, gently grasp a bit of hair between your thumb and index finger in a manner that allows you to gently pull the loose hairs away from the rabbit's body. Try to keep your fingers at the outside edges, or tips, of the hair. Since it's the longest hair that is releasing, you will have an easier time pulling if you are only grabbing the very ends of the hair. If you try to pull hair from its middle or close to the skin, you're likely to be tugging on hair that isn't ready to shed. You won't successfully take any hair off. And your bunny will be annoyed.

Here I am, plucking wool from Spinner. It looks like I'm pulling the poor thing's ears off! In fact, I'm gently holding and occasionally stroking her head and ears.

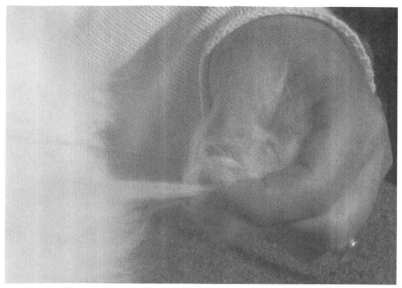

Pull small sections of wool at a time. I stop to rest my fingers from time to time, otherwise my muscles get cramped.

- Not sure which areas you've harvested and which need work? Pause and take a look at your rabbit. Can you see the difference in color and texture between the hair that is loose and ready for removal and the hair that remains in the area you've plucked? On colored rabbits, the hair left behind in plucked areas will be shorter and darker. Light colored tufts of long hair will remain in the areas yet unharvested. This visual difference in the coat will help guide you. White rabbits are more difficult to judge visually – but by locating the areas of comparatively short hair, you'll be able to determine where you've already worked.

- Work your way systematically across the bunny's body, harvesting sections so you can easily see what areas have been plucked and what areas will need to be addressed in a later harvesting session. Often, a rabbit will blow its coat from the top of its body down. You can go ahead and pluck the neck, back, sides and butt area first. It's perfectly fine to leave the rest for a few days. Your bunny will look like it has a "dust ruffle" along the bottom half of its body.

There's a marked difference between the light-colored fiber I'm harvesting and the shorter, darker new coat left behind on Cap'n Jack's back.

• Come back to the bunny a few days later to continue the plucking process. Again, start with a complete comb through to loosen the hairs and determine which areas are ready to release wool.

• If you have English or English X angoras, you'll need to pluck the wool on the legs, stomach, face and feet of your bunny. The wool from this part of the body is fairly short. Many folks don't use it at all and simply discard it. I find it useful for stuffing, felting and as test material for dyeing. Access the stomach and feet in whichever manner works best for you. Be sure to leave a protective layer of fur on the bottom of the rabbit's feet.

General Directions for Shearing

- Gather your shearing tools – a comb or grooming rake and the scissors that you use ONLY for shearing your rabbit(s). Be sure your scissors are clean, disinfected and sharp. Many owners utilize scissors with blunt, rounded ends to insure they won't cut the rabbit accidentally.

- Work with your bunny on your lap, a table or grooming stand – whichever feels most comfortable to you. Administer a preliminary "comb through" with a steel comb or grooming rake. This will untangle the rabbit's coat and make working in sections of hair much easier and quicker.

- Starting at the top of your rabbit's back, take a small section of hair into your non-dominant hand. Slide the scissors into place behind the section of hair, resting on the rabbit's body. Rotate the scissors so the blades are perpendicular to the rabbit's skin (at a 90 degree angle).

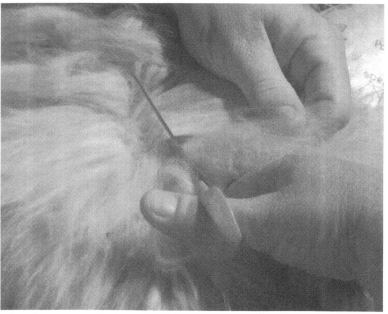

The first cut of fiber, showing position of scissors at the base of the rabbit's wool.

The rotation of the blades insures that there will be space between the blades and the body of the rabbit– and you won't cut your rabbit (see photo). You really won't! Now cut through that section of hair, lift it away from rabbit's body and place in a box, bag or basket.

• Pick up a section of hair adjacent to the area you just cut and repeat the above process. It doesn't matter which direction you decide to go, as long as you continue taking small sections of hair, cutting, and then taking the adjacent section of hair. I typically work across the rabbit's back from the neck to the butt or start in the middle of the rabbit's back and work from the top down each side of the rabbit's body.

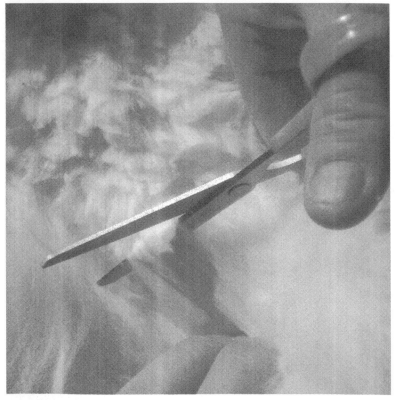

Work your way along the rabbit's body, shearing small sections of wool.

- At first, the shearing process will go slowly for you. That's just fine! Take your time. There's no need to shear the entire rabbit in one session. It's best if you allow yourself and your rabbit a few shorter sessions in which to get used to the experience of shearing. In time, you'll gain confidence and feel more at ease with the scissors. Your rabbit will become comfortable as well. The less fidgeting, the better, where scissors are involved!

- Shear your rabbit completely, so that all long fiber has been removed. On French, Satin and crossbreeds, you will only need to shear your rabbit's back, sides, butt and chest. On English and English X breeds, you will also need to shear the tummy, feet, legs and face. Regardless of breed, your rabbit will look quite humorous when you are finished. It will have a very short layer of wool all over, but will still look ... well, naked. Bet you had no idea what a tiny rabbit was lurking under all that fluff!

Chris Morgan's buck, Bunjamin Braddock, just after a shearing.

Make a Bunny Cozy!

Shearing leaves a bunny with quite a short coat. If there is chilly weather, you'll want to provide your rabbit with extra warmth until his or her fluff gets longer. Knit up a little tube (ribbing is good for easy sizing) with holes for bunny's front feet. Or... stitch together a tiny fleece jacket. Fleece is inexpensive, very warm, easy to sew by hand and available at most fabric and craft stores. Another quick bunny cozy can be made by purchasing a wool sweater at a thrift store. (My bunny, Odie, demonstrates below.) Wash in the washing machine and run through the dryer to felt it. Cut off one of the arms to an appropriate length. Slip on to bunny with wrist ribbing at the neck. Take note of where bunny's feet need to come through. Cut holes. Voila! Is it just too kooky for an angora rabbit to wear a wool, alpaca or cashmere cozy? I think not!

Odie shows off her new wool cozy... Much warmer now, thanks!

The Nervous New Owner's Guide to **Angora Rabbits**

Shearing with Clippers

If you have several rabbits (or very little time!), consider investing in a set of electric grooming clippers. Shearing with clippers is fast. Incredibly fast. It also nullifies the please-oh-please-don't-let-me-nip-the-bunny anxiety that even the most seasoned scissor-shearer feels. Purchase a good quality set of clippers, made for use with angora rabbits. Prepare yourself to spend $300 to $400 right from the start. The angora rabbit community most often recommends the Aesculap or "German Red Clipper", available at specialty animal supply stores and online. There are several versions (cordless, corded, with multiple blades, etc.) and the clippers come with a warrantee. German Red Clippers were developed specifically for production shearing of angora rabbits. You can also peruse online discussions for additional brands of clippers that may be a bit less expensive but still adequate to the job. Owners and breeders like to keep each other updated when they discover new, trustworthy tools.

Katie Musante's bunny Cooley, looks smooth, smooth, smooth after a shearing with electric clippers.

As the Fluff Comes Off...

Take some time before harvesting to think about what you will do with angora wool as it comes off your rabbit. It's best to set up your system ahead of time, rather than running around trying to get organized with a bunny in hand! Depending upon your personality, available time and end-use of the fiber you collect, you're likely to employ one of the following two approaches. I have no judgments on which is better -- but I'll admit that I'm an admirer of the first approach and a practitioner of the second!

The Organize-As-You-Go Approach

(For those who prefer to evaluate and separate out the angora wool as it is harvested...)

For this approach, you will need to have multiple containers on-hand as you begin to harvest your rabbit. As each tuft comes off the rabbit, identify whether it is prime fiber, secondary fiber or discards. Make sure you keep these different fibers separate from each other as you harvest. For prime fiber, you'll want a hard-sided container. Try using a shoebox, clear plastic clamshell (i.e. portable food storage container, usually seen at salad bars and the ready made food section of your grocery store), lidded plastic storage bin, photo box or covered basket. As you harvest, place the prime locks carefully in the hard-sided container. Lay the fibers parallel to each other, in a single layer, all the way across the container. Once you have a first layer of fibers, place tissue paper or paper towels. Then begin placing the next layer of parallel fibers on top. Repeat until container is full. The alternating layers of paper and fiber make it easier for you to pick up the wool later. They also help keep the contents from condensing down due to weight. You want to keep your prime locks lofty and full of air. Be sure to add a note with information regarding the particular rabbit, date of harvest and any other information that might be useful. Why add in the note? Because though you think you'll remember everything about this fiber just by looking at it later, you won't. Trust me on this one. Write it down. Anything that doesn't qualify as prime fiber can be stored in a labeled container or bag. Discards get thrown into yet a third container and will be taken later to the trash or compost heap.

Advantage(s): Later, you can just pick up the angora harvest and start working with the wool without having to do any further preparation.

Disadvantage(s): Lengthens harvesting sessions, requires a fair amount of equipment to be on hand and can distract you from paying attention to the rabbit. Also, rabbits do get fidgety when you are fussing with wool instead of with them.

The I'll-Deal-With-It-Later Approach

(For those who prefer to concentrate on harvesting the wool as quickly as possible...)

For this approach, you'll only need one container. As you pluck or shear, place all fiber into a bag, box or basket. Cover or close the container. Put it away until you are ready to work with the harvested fiber. That's it – the entire process!

Advantage(s): Keeps harvesting sessions shorter, allows you to concentrate on the act of plucking or shearing and you won't hear your rabbit exclaim "Ahem... over here. Stop gazing at my beautiful locks and get on with it!"

Disadvantage(s): Later, when you'd rather be spinning, blending or felting with your harvested fiber, you'll have to take time to skirt, comb and/or card the harvested wool before you can play with it.

Fiber Prep

If you've collected a nice harvest of angora wool, by now you are more than ready to put it to use. This next step, where your home-grown fiber is transformed into a usable material, is referred to as "fiber prep". Fiber prep results in yarn -- for knitting, crocheting and weaving. Or, it can result in clean, raw fiber – for use in spinning and felting.

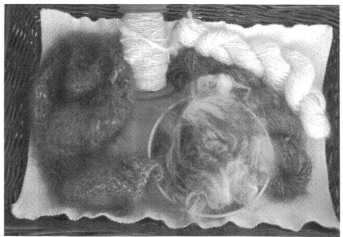

Angora fiber in an assortment of forms: a knitted scarf, a bobbin of handspun yarn, a bowl of raw fiber ready for spinning or felting, and two skeins of 100% angora yarn.

The Nervous New Owner's Guide to **Angora Rabbits**

Depending upon your interest level, tools at hand and available time, you can do the fiber prep yourself. Conversely, you can choose to send your harvested wool out to a mill for processing. And if your intention is to felt with or spin 100% angora wool, you will have very little to do before your fiber is ready for the work at hand. However, you may want to consider taking the time to blend your angora wool with a second fiber.

Most "angora" yarn that you see at yarn stores and fiber festivals is a blend of angora rabbit and sheep's wool (or increasingly, alpaca). You may choose to create a similar blended yarn or roving for your own use.

A skein of Jolene Richardson's handspun angora/cashmere blended yarn.

Blending has two advantages. First, it "stretches" your angora into greater amounts of usable finished product. Angora yarn/ roving will typically be blended at 10-50% angora with the remaining amount in the added fiber. You've just doubled, tripled or quadrupled the amount of "angora yarn" produced. Second, blending introduces the qualities of second (and sometimes third and fourth!) fiber to your finished yarn – qualities that angora yarn by itself does not have. Sheep's wool and alpaca bring a capacity for "memory" (a garment can be stretched, tugged and worn but will snap back into its original shape without staying permanently stretched) and loft to your yarn. Silk and cellulose fibers (i.e. rayon, etc.) introduce a lovely sheen and help the finished material drape well. The yarn produced will exhibit the qualities of the angora wool or the second fiber or both, depending upon the proportions used. The decision to blend fiber will increase the time involved with fiber prep. You may also have to add a few items to your collection of fiber tools. (Oh, darn!)

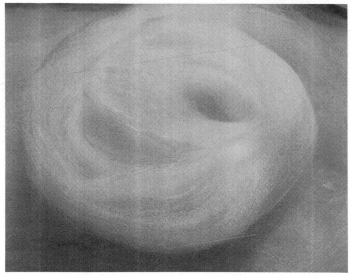

A swirl of Jolene Richardson's lovely Angel Blend: merino, angora, soy and bamboo. Yum!

If your intent is to work with the angora fiber from your rabbit's body to finished garment, then you'll enjoy the time and activity involved with blending. However, if the fiber prep becomes tedious -- or you'd rather use that time to spin, knit or weave -- feel free to hand off your angora harvest to a mill (wool processing facility). You send them your raw fiber. They send back beautiful, clean, blended roving or finished yarn. Using a mill for fiber prep starts looking like a very good idea when you have limited time and/or multiple rabbits!

Mill Processing

There are now several mills across the country with the equipment necessary to process angora wool. You will see them advertising the capability to work with "specialty" fibers such as angora, silk, dog and cat hair and other "exotic" animal fibers. To have a mill process your angora, gather your wool and sort out any too-short or stained fiber. Make sure you've removed any vegetable matter, such as straw or shavings, that may be caught in the wool. Bag up the wool and compress it in order to send it in as small a box as possible.

Next, pull out your phone. Call the mill. Talk with one of their representatives regarding the following subjects:

• The type, amount and character of the fiber you have.

• The finished product you'd like to receive. Ask about their process for getting your raw wool to that finished product.

• The final cost, how it's determined and when you will need to pay for the mill's services.

• The estimated length of time (usually called "lead time") before you can expect to receive your finished product.

Take notes during the conversation. Date your notes. Be sure to get the name of the person with whom you are speaking. If anything goes awry with your order, this information will be very helpful for both you and the mill.

Can't find the information listed above on the mill's website or published brochures? Why yes, you can. But when you are sending your fiber to a mill for the first few times, it's best to invest some time in creating a relationship with the mill staff. Introduce yourself. Ask a lot of questions – they won't mind and it's in your best interest to do so. Hold them responsible for what they promise to do for you. If possible, always work with the same representative from the mill. After a while, you'll have developed a friendly rapport. The mill staff will trust you; you'll trust the mill staff. And you'll be able to send your fiber off with very little fuss, simply letting them know your sending some out for "the usual".

Wool processing mills are primarily small, family-owned businesses. They care about their clients and the quality of the work produced. It's important that they maintain a good reputation with the fiber community. If ever a problem does arise, give them the chance to make it right before you go making some hysterical post online. I guarantee you the mill is interested in correcting whatever mishap has occurred rather than having you out there bashing their good name. Also, mill owners are just plain old nice folks.

Do-It-Yourself Fiber Prep

If you love handling fiber in general, especially this wonderfully soft, light angora wool you've harvested, you might well enjoy the fiber prep best of all! There's something relaxing and satisfying about the physical act of preparing fiber for use. With a little elbow grease, you turn a slightly messy, unorganized pile of fluff into a nice, clean pile of fiber waiting to be put into use. It's much like straightening up the kitchen and gathering all your ingredients prior to cooking up a favorite recipe. Ah, anticipation! While you work you'll be thinking of all the lovely things you're going to make with this angora...

Now if you harvested in the Organize-As-You-Go approach, you might not have much fiber prep to do at all. Take out that container of perfectly laid out, prime fiber. There, your prep is done! You can get right to spinning or felting. Unless you'd like to blend that fiber with some wool or alpaca, which means you need to do a little bit more prep. But we'll get to that in a moment.

If, however, you used the I'll-Deal-With-It-Later approach (as I do), you have a few steps ahead of you before you can get to spinning or felting. First, dump that fiber out onto a table and start evaluating the lot. Pull out anything you know is too short, stained or matted to be included. Send it straight to the trash or compost heap. Next, you'll want to do three things: align the fibers so they are all going in one direction, separate out any remaining short fibers, and get the angora wool as fluffy and light as possible.

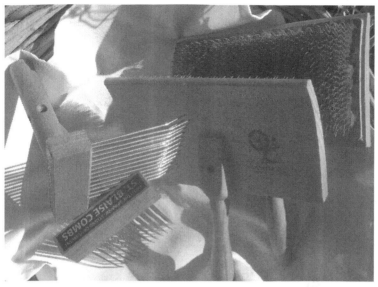

For comparison: a pair of combs (left) and carders (right).

Crafters use two tools to prepare fiber for spinning: carders and combs. Carders, also called "wool carders" or "hand carders" are wide, flat, paddle-like tools with steel-toothed cloth adhered to the interior surface of each. You *can* use them to prep your angora, if you desire. They will achieve two of the three desired ends: aligning the fibers and getting your angora fluffy and light. However, I recommend working with combs instead.

Wool combs resemble large, steel-toothed grooming rakes. But don't use them on your bunnies! They are designed to prepare fiber for spinning. The advantage in using them is that they allow you to separate out the short, unusable fibers from the longer, prime fibers you want to use. Combs are my my personal choice for fiber preparation because I toss all my harvested fiber into one bin for later "attention".

When choosing combs, look for a set made specifically for work with fine fibers. You'll see them referred to as "mini-combs". The tines (steel spikes) on mini-combs are closer together and shorter than those on combs made for use with sheep's wool. But don't be fooled by the use of the term "mini"! To process your angora, you will still require a nice, heavy duty tool. Look for solid wood construction, a hefty handle and tines heavier than any of your grooming combs. If you purchase a set of combs which are too lightweight, you'll find yourself replacing them within a year. For recommendations on specific manufacturers of mini-combs,

For comparison: one each from a set of Louet mini-combs (double row), St. Blaise mini-combs (double row) and Indigo Hound combs (single row, primarily for use with wool).

scroll through some online discussions about fiber prep. Or, post your own specific request for recommendations from other angora owners. You'll get very honest replies about the variety of tools in current use – as well as strong opinions concerning which ones hold up well and which do not!

Combing Angora

To comb angora fiber, you'll want to have three containers on hand -- one to hold raw fiber, one for combed fluff and somewhere to put your short/discarded fiber. I also keep my secret weapon for preventing static within arm's reach: a spray bottle filled with water, a few drops of jojoba oil and 2-3 drops of essential oil. It's hard enough to keep the fluff from getting everywhere; an occasional spray really helps! Then grab your combs and you're ready to start.

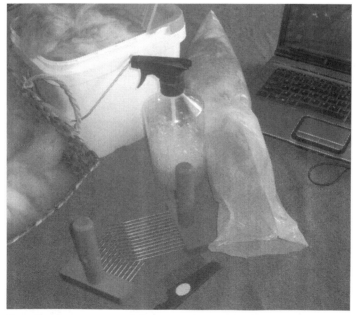

Ready for my combing session! Did I mention the importance of a computer? I listen to music or an audiobook while working.

Combing angora fiber is a bit different than combing other types of wool, as it doesn't require as many passes. Just a few will straighten and separate fibers sufficiently. I have a particular system that I use for combing. Try mine or feel free to experiment with varying techniques until you find what is most comfortable and effective for you.

- First, grasp a handful of the raw wool in your dominant hand and pick up one of the combs with your other hand.

- "Charge" the comb – which means place the wool onto the empty comb. You can do this by carefully bringing the outside edge of your clump of wool down over the tines of the combs. Keep your fingers well out of the way! The comb will hold on to a few of the fibers as you pass by. Then repeat, catching a little more. Keep charging the comb until you have the whole clump of angora wool on the comb. Once I have the comb fully loaded, I give it two or three spritzes with my anti-static formula.

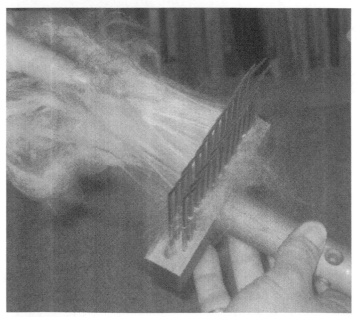

Charging the comb. Watch those fingers!

- Pick up your other comb. With the empty comb in your dominant hand, brush by the charged comb at a right angle, touching just the tips of the fiber. Your empty comb should pick up some of the wool. Now repeat, going a little deeper into the charged comb's fiber as you pass by. The fiber will be a bit wet because of the anti-static spray. Don't worry. By the time you finish combing, it will be dry but not flying all over. Try to remember to keep both combs pointing away from you. I tend to start combing in all sorts of odd directions and only become aware of it when I jab myself! Complete a few more passes with the comb until you aren't drawing off any more fiber and what remains looks well combed.

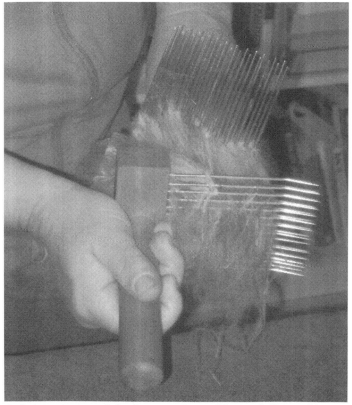

A few passes with the combs will straighten fibers and sort out short, unusable bits.

- Put down one of the combs. With one hand, hold the comb up. With the other hand, grasp a small section of combed fiber and pull loose from the comb. It's a bit like plucking a section of hair off your rabbit.

Grasp a bit of the combed fiber and pull a perfectly beautiful tuft of angora fiber off those combs.

As the bit comes loose, lay it down in a waiting box, basket or bowl. Repeat until you have taken all the long fibers off this comb. Then pick up the other comb and do a few passes on the fiber it's holding. When it looks sufficiently combed, pull those fibers off as well. You should have a nice pile of fluffy, combed angora wool in your container.

- Pull the remaining, short and tangled fibers off your combs. You can discard these remains. I keep them and use them for felting or stuffing.

- Continue the process with your combs and the pile of raw angora fiber until you've combed through the lot.

If you plan to spin your prepared fiber right away, you don't need to layer it with paper to retain the loft. It won't have time to compress. If you are going to store the fiber for later use, though, go ahead and store it in a hard-sided container, with paper, as described in the "Organize As You Go" approach to harvesting.

The Nervous New Owner's Guide to **Angora Rabbits**

A basket full of combed fiber, ready for spinning!

Do-It-Yourself Blending

Blending fiber can be done on either a set of carders or combs or by using a drum carder. The idea is to work two types of wool together, creating a third fiber that offers the qualities of both. No matter what tools you use to do the actual blending, you'll first need to decide upon the desired proportions of angora to the secondary wool. Again, it is rare to find an angora blend that is more than 50% angora. In fact, incorporating as little as 10% angora into a secondary wool will add the softness and halo that is so beloved by knitters and spinners. Experiment with your first few batches to see what appeals to you. If you know the intended use of the blended yarn, it will also help you to determine what proportions you'd like to incorporate. Garments like sweaters and vests are best with a low proportion of angora wool, to maintain visible stitch work and prevent the item from becoming too warm for wear. Items like shawls, mittens and hats can typically include higher proportions of angora.

Once you've decided on your proportions, set yourself up to work so that you have all the necessary angora and secondary wool ready for blending.

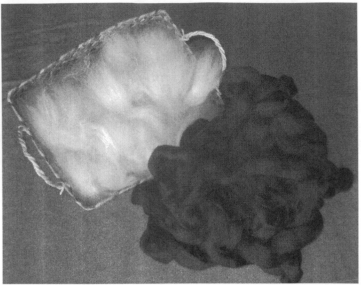

The same basket of combed angora alongside some commercially prepared black wool roving. Blended together, they will create a yarn that is 10% angora and 90% wool.

- But where, oh where, to start? I like to get my fiber ready for blending by dividing it into small, proportioned and easily stored batches. That way I won't have fluff all over the house when I want to do some blending. I can just take out a small bag and start!

- First, separate your angora fluff into eight or ten piles. Next, take the secondary fiber and add it in sections to the small angora piles – in the proportions needed. I weighed my wool and found it was 22 oz. Then I collected 2.2 oz. from my prepared angora. You can "eyeball" the proportions when separating and get pretty close to the intended percentages. Or, if you prefer to be more exact, use a small scale.

Piles of angora fluff and wool roving, in the correct proportions, are ready for blending or storage.

• Are your piles small enough to work with, or should you further divide them? If you decide to divide, be sure you create smaller piles with exactly the same proportions of each fiber (i.e. divide your angora in half, divide your merino in half, recombine into two smaller piles).

• Place individual bundles of angora and wool in bags (I use Ziplock sandwich bags) until you are ready to work with them.

Now you can begin blending! If you are using combs or carders to blend, simply "charge" your tools from your small pile of both fibers. Work back and forth from comb to comb or carder to carder until you see the fibers are sufficiently blended.

If you have a great deal of fiber to blend, you might consider adding a drum carder to your fiber equipment. A drum carder blends large amounts of fiber quickly and with relatively little effort -- especially if you happen to purchase a motorized one. Be sure to get a "fine" drum carder, or one that allows you to change the carding cloth for use with fine fibers.

Here's my Fancy Kitty drum carder after I've put the angora and wool through for the first pass. Looks a bit like Cruella De Vil's hair! Just a few more times through the carder will result in a thorough meld.

Blend with your drum carder by slowly feeding in your proportioned piles of wool. Make sure you are introducing both wools to the width of the carder as well as along the length of the drum as you feed. Check the batts carefully as they come off the carder to see if you are blending adequately. It will take several passes to achieve a good blend. Remove finished batts and set them aside for use as soon as you've blended all the fiber in your piles. Or, if you are like me – and get very excited about things – run over to your spinning wheel and try out your fiber right away!

Tips and Techniques

Dyeing

Angora fiber takes dye beautifully! Treat yourself to some experimentation in this area of fiber fun. You will love the results. The angora wool can be dyed straight off the bunny, as loose fiber. Dyeing loose fiber allows you to spin different colors together, creating variegated yarn. Or, you can spin up your angora into yarn and dye the skeins. Skeins can be dyed with a single color, dipped, spattered or brushed with dyes to introduce variegation. Use dyes and dye processes appropriate for protein fibers (i.e. sheep's wool, alpaca, bison, etc. as opposed to cellulose fibers like cotton, rayon and linen).

Two things to keep in mind about your angora that will help you achieve a good outcome:

- Beware of **felting your fiber** while dying. Angora is very susceptible. Keep any temperature changes very, very gradual. Moving quickly from hot liquid to a cold rinse is the worst perpetrator! Rather, try removing fibers from a hot dye bath and letting them cool in a bowl or sink before rinsing clear. Agitation will also induce felting. Move the fiber as little as possible while in the dye bath.

- Angora takes **a long time to absorb moisture**. On rabbits, that is a wonderful, protective characteristic of their coat. For dyeing, it's a little problematic. Most dye processes will require that your fiber is pre-moistened before immersing in the color. You will need to soak your angora fiber for several hours in order to make sure it is completely wet. I soak mine for a full day before dyeing with it. I also submerge my hands into the soaking angora and gently squeeze the fibers, releasing any trapped air (especially when soaking loose fiber). I do this a few different times while the fiber is soaking, just to be sure I've touched every area of the submerged fiber.

For the brightest, most pure color effects, dye with white angora fiber. I like to include some grey and tan angora fibers in with the white. The muting of the color on the darker fibers creates a lovely variegation within the same color along the length of the yarn as you spin it. Dyed angora fiber is also a treat to blend in with secondary wools. You can also spin a length of dyed angora fiber and then ply it with a length of commercially dyed yarn. The possibilities for color and texture are endless.

Spinning

Two topics repeatedly arise when the subject of spinning angora comes up. One is the long-held (and inaccurate, darn it!) belief that angora wool is hard to spin. I've heard countless folks, even within the fiber community, repeat that fiction. Let me say right now, for the record, that spinning angora is not difficult.

I mean it. **Not difficult!**

It's just a little different than spinning wool. I suspect that folks say angora is hard to spin because they get used to spinning one type of fiber and then are surprised when their techniques don't work on another. Each fiber has its own properties and requires a unique approach. Angora is no more difficult to spin than mohair, silk, soy, tencel or any other material that differs in texture from sheep's wool.

Learning to spin angora can be approached just like learning to spin in general. Start slowly. Get a feel for how the material draws from your hands. Experiment with techniques and thicknesses. Resign yourself to the fact that your first efforts will be far from perfect. (Look for a project that incorporates very bumpy, uneven yarn!) In a very short time, you will find yourself spinning away with your angora as if you'd been doing it for years.

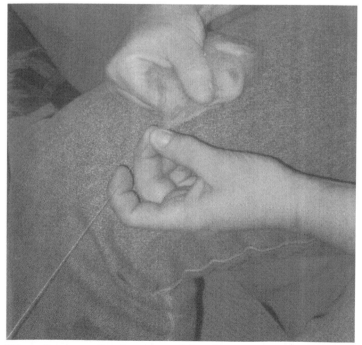

Here I am, spinning up a bit of lovely, static-free angora from the day's earlier combing session.

The second topic that comes up repeatedly is spinning equipment. Yes, you can spin angora on a drop spindle. I've seen it done. I've done it myself. Spindles are a great tool for fiber folks on the go. Use a spindle on the lighter side of the spectrum, as you are likely to make a fine yarn and the fiber itself doesn't weigh much. Spindles come in a variety of shapes and sizes and are now made out of quite interesting materials, including cds, stone donuts, metal and glass. Even the more traditional spindles, crafted from wood, are embellished with beautiful inlay, painted motifs and carvings. And if you are thinking about getting a spinning wheel, know that all types of wheels can spin angora fiber – portables, Saxony, castle, modern, spindle and electric. I've come to understand that it's not *what* you are spinning on but rather *how* you spin that is at the heart of the matter.

A basket of combed angora, a fire in the wood stove, your dog at your side and a bit of free time to spin... What could be better?

Finishing (aka "Wet Finishing" or "Fulling") Your Angora Yarn

Finishing is the most important step when spinning with angora. This finishing process is called "fulling". I feel it is essential to a high quality angora yarn. You will need the following supplies: a squirt of liquid dish soap, sink or large bowl, a potato masher or sink plunger, cold water and a towel or salad spinner.

- Fill your bowl with very hot water, add a squirt of detergent and then add your tied skein of angora yarn.

- Use the potato masher or sink plunger to compress the skein (push down , squeezing out all trapped air).

- Dump out the hot water and fill the bowl with cold water. (Now is a good time to re-align the skein to prevent tangles.)

- Fill up your bowl with hot water and compress it over and over until the water is clear of soap residue.

- Dump the hot and add cold water again to completely rinse the soap out of the skein. At this time I add a splash of white vinegar to help remove the soap. After your first try, you will learn how much soap to use based on how many times you have to rinse.

- I do a final hot rinse and add one or two drops of essential oil to the skein to mask out any vinegar scent.

- Use a towel or salad spinner to remove the excess water.

- Now it is time to whack the skein. Re-align the skein, hold one end of the skein and give the other end a hard whack against your counter top. Turn it around and give it another whack. Whacking opens up the fibers and helps the yarn develop its famous "halo".

(Excerpted from Christine Durkin's website at WeSpinAngora.com. Thanks, Christine!)

Yarn Notes

A single strand (or "ply") of 100% angora fiber will be a bit precarious when put to use. Though the prime fibers from your rabbit should be long enough to stay put in your spun yarn, you'll want to lock them in place by plying. I suggest plying all angora yarn, but especially that made only of angora wool. In fact, when I spin up 100% angora, I usually Navajo ply – which creates a three ply yarn. If you start with a very fine single, the Navajo ply comes out to be a mid-weight yarn with great strength and superb halo.

A very popular way to make "blended" yarn (without having to blend!) is to ply a single of 100% angora with a single (or multiples) of a secondary fiber. Favorite ply partners include silk, merino, suri and huacaya alpaca, soy fibers and tencel.

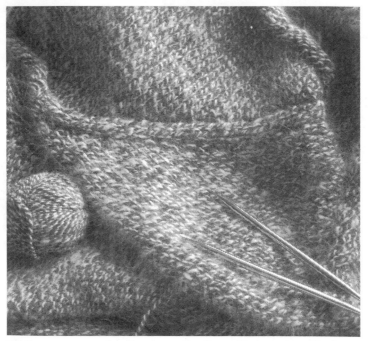

This yarn -- a single strand of 100% angora plied with a strand of commercial silk/wool blend -- will make a luscious sweater.

A note on joining yarn end to end: Angora yarn and angora/ protein fiber blend yarns can be spit-spliced together. In fact, this kind of joint is preferable to a tied connection as there are no loose ends left around just waiting to un-spin themselves into oblivion.

Knit, Crochet and Felting Notes

Making something (anything!) out of your own home-grown angora yarn is pure pleasure. Not only is it lovely to handle, it's immensely satisfying to hold the knowledge that the yarn was made from your own animals and efforts while you work with it. Garments made from angora are exceptionally soft, light and warm. Consider making items that are small and protective for the body. Scarves, mittens, fingerless gloves, leg warmers and hats make wonderful gifts. They also put your soft angora yarn right next to someone's skin – the best place for it!

When knitting or crocheting an item, you'll notice it develop a network of loose, fluffy fibers along the surface. That phenomenon is called the angora "halo". The halo is part of what makes angora desirable as a soft, comfortable fiber for use in garments. Not only does it look wonderfully comforting, the fiber's halo fills in the space around loose stitches and between open ones. The tiny fibers trap air, creating a layer of insulation between the skin and the temperatures outside the body. Angora wool is so highly insulating, it can sometimes be too warm for comfort. A garment that will cover a large portion of the body (i.e. a sweater) is best made from a blended yarn. You don't want your gift recipients to complain of overheating!

Are you working a project with intricate stitches? Consider using a blended angora yarn and stay away from a too-tight gauge. Otherwise, the halo of the yarn will obscure much of what you are doing in your pattern. To get a better effect, switch to a larger set of needles/hook. The more loosely the fabric is knit or crocheted, the better your stitches can be seen. In fact, angora yarn, both blended and pure, works very well for light, lacy patterns. The more lace or "open" stitch work you incorporate, the more visible the stitch work will be.

A knitted cowl by Katie Musante (above) and Jolene Richardson's beautiful lacework (below) in angora yarn. All from their own rabbits!

Be sure to block your finished project to open up all the stitches and show the patterns. You can block angora yarn by completely wetting it and then pinning in place to dry. If you prefer to steam block, protect the angora yarn by placing a towel between the iron and the project as you work.

Felted angora makes wonderfully soft garments, bags and housewares. To felt with angora, work as you would with wool. The fibers don't lock together quite as easily; it may take additional agitation to get the felting as dense as you'd like. You can also create a base layer of felted wool, then add angora on top. In this manner, the bulk of your felted item is made from a less expensive material but still has the soft angora for the surface color and texture.

Washing

Wash angora garments with very mild soap. Any liquid castile soap (like Dr. Bronner's), low sudsing olive-oil based bar soap or detergent-free dishwashing liquid will do. Add the soap to a sink full of cold water, swish around a bit to disperse and then submerge your garment into the liquid. Gently press down with your hands to release any trapped air bubbles. Remember, angora takes a long time to get fully wet. You'll need to soak the item in the soapy water for twice as long (or longer) than you'd leave a wool or silk garment. After sufficient soaking, release the water and rinse in water that is room temperature. Don't wring! Instead, wrap the garment in a towel and gently press the excess water out. Lay out flat to dry. The halo will reappear as soon as the garment is dry and has been handled a bit.

Resources

Books

Completely Angora
By Sharon Kilfoyle and Leslie B. Samson
Published by Samson Angoras, Ontario, Canada.
The BIBLE for angora rabbit owners! Out of print, now, which means it can be hard to find. Check with online angora groups to see if anyone has a copy they are willing to lend or sell to you.

Angora, A Handbook for Spinners
By Erica Lynne
Published by Interweave Press
A nice little tome on our furry friends and how to use their wool.

Rabbits for Dummies
By Audrey Pavia
Published by Wiley Publishing, Inc.
A great intro book for the novice owner. Easy to read, full of good information and not too intimidating. One of the first books I read as a rabbit owner.

Storey's Guide to Raising Rabbits
By Bob Bennett
Published by Storey Publishing
Storey Publishing is THE BOMB (uh, that's a good thing, according to my teenagers...) when it comes to providing useful and very complete information on how to do anything yourself -- whether it's gardening, working with animals, making clothes, building accessory buildings or cleaning with natural products. I love their books. This one is a very useful reference.

Raising Rabbits
By Ann Kanable
Published by Rodale Press
While I thought this would be "just another rabbit book" when I picked it up, I quickly found myself drawn into the useful and delightfully surprising information offered up by the author. A great one for your library – I highly recommend it.

Don't Shoot the Dog! The New Art of Teaching and Training
By Karen Pryor
Published by Bantam Books
The classic work on training animals via behavioral conditioning. Sure, she talks about her work with dolphins. But all the principals translate to rabbits, as well as dogs, teenagers, spouses, co-workers. Useful in so many ways!

The Self-Publishing Manual
By Dan Poynter
Published by Para Publishing
Gotta give credit where credit is due. Without this book, THIS book would never have come into being. Thanks, Dan, for the information and encouragement you provide to all potential authors.

Online Communities/Discussion Groups

Ravelry.com
Ravelry is a free site online for knitters and crocheters. You send a request to join. Once a member, you have access to a universe of patterns, discussion groups, events... oh, it goes on and on! Anyone interested in fiber at all will love this site. The angora rabbit discussion there can be found at
www.ravelry.com/groups/angora-rabbits

Yahoo.com
All you need to join one of the thousands of group discussions on yahoo.com is an email address with them. There are groups on each breed of angora, one specifically for owners of fiber rabbits and one for general discussion about angora rabbits. You can find the general angora discussion at
http://pets.groups.yahoo.com/group/AngoraRabbitList/

Useful Web Sites (listed in no particular order!)

**The International Association
of German Angora Rabbit Breeders (IAGARB)**
www.iagarb.com
A powerhouse of a website, packed with information that is appropriate for owners of all breeds of angora rabbits.

Petfinder.com
A great online site which posts pictures and descriptions of adoptable animals at shelters, rescue groups and humane societies across the country. Search by animal type and breed to come up with any angora rabbits in need of a home.

Quality Cage Company and **Woody's Wabbits**
Both are highly recommended, have loyal fans and are located in Oregon. Is there some secret ingredient in the Oregon air???
www.qualitycage.com
www.woodyswabbits.com

BunnyRabbit.Com
Another AMAZING website, full of articles, pictures and every item you could ever want in relation to your bunny rabbit. Located in San Antonio, Texas... serving everywhere.
www.bunnyrabbit.com

Bass Equipment Company
Great equipment from a longstanding company.
www.bassequipment.com

Ebay
You'll be amazed by the equipment and hutch options found here. Check it out.
www.ebay.com

Fiber Festivals

This is by no means a complete list of fiber festivals! It is, however, a list of the larger, more well-known ones. There are are numerous regional fiber festivals and gatherings that are well worth attending -- and are often less overwhelming than the "biggies" listed below. However, I absolutely KNOW you will find angora rabbits for sale at any of these events.

April
Connecticut Sheep, Wool and Fiber Festival
(Vernon/Rockville, CT)

May
Maryland Sheep and Wool Festival (West Friendship, MA)

June
Black Sheep Gathering (Eugene, OR)

September
Oregon Flock and Fiber Festival (Canby, OR)
Wisconsin Sheep and Wool Festival (Jefferson, WI)

October
New York State Sheep and Wool Festival (Rhinebeck, NY)
Southeastern Animal Fiber Fair (Asheville, NC)
Taos Wool Festival (Taos, NM)
Vermont Sheep and Wool Festival (Tunbridge, VT)

A Short Glossary of Terms

buck: a male rabbit

crimp: tiny waves visible along the length of angora fiber (which look like they could have been put in place with a very small crimping iron!)

doe: a female rabbit

furnishings: tufts of wool that grow on the ears, face and feet of English angoras

guard hair: heavy, coarse hair present on a rabbit to separate and protect the softer, more desirable undercoat

halo: a fluffy, fuzzy surface created by individual ends of angora hairs disengaging from the twist in yarn

hand: the feel, or texture, of a particular material

kit: a baby rabbit

loft: air present among and between fibers resulting in lighter weight and density

memory: elasticity; the ability of a material to snap back into shape after being stretched out

roving: a long, narrow bundle of fiber that has been cleaned and prepared for use in spinning, felting or other craft endeavors

skein: a quantity of yarn wound in a long, loose coil

Contributors

Why is the Resources section of the book printed in such small type? So I could have room to credit these folks!!! What a wonderful group of individuals. They sent me pictures, read through drafts, notified me when I was off my rocker (in very gentle terms, I must say...) and convinced me that someone out there would want to buy this book.

Thank you, all of you, from the bottom of my heart.

Betsy Bailey
Sticks and Spokes
Salem, Oregon
Ravelry: lizzibet

Deb Boyken
www.knittingscholar.com
New Jersey
Ravelry: chappysmom

Christine Durkin
We Spin Angora
Gainesville, Georgia
www.wespinangora.com
Ravelry: xine

Rebecca Gould
Angora Amora
Jeffersonville, Indiana
www.angoraamora.blogspot.com
www.angoraamora.etsy.com
Ravelry: angoraamora

Susan Helgeson
Houston, TX
Ravelry: fourbears

Penelope Hemingway
York, North Yorkshire, UK
www.theknittinggenealogist.
wordpress.com
Ravelry: penelopespider
That's her grandmother's cousin in the photo on page 39. It's the oldest known photograph of angora rabbits in the UK. So awesome!

Betty and Jenny Moon
AngoraMoon Rabbitry
www.angoramoon.com
www.angoramoon.info
Deming, New Mexico
Ravelry: mysticklobo, craftywabbit

Chris Morgan
Woolybuns Rabbitry
Connecticut
Ravelry: woolybuns

Katie Musante
High Desert Fiberworks &
Spun Buns Angora Rabbits
Central Oregon
www.highdesertfiberworks.com
www.spunbuns.etsy.com
Ravelry: oregonrose

Pam Ramsey
La Plata Farms
Hesperus, Colorado
www.laplatafarms.com
Ravelry: churromom

Franco Rios
Sacramento, California
www.rabbitgeek.com
Ravelry: francorios
Weavolution: francorios

Dawn Rzeszot
Furry Face Fibers
Fort Edward, NY
Ravelry: crochettreasures

Jolene Richardson
Jobo Designs
Cornwall, Prince Edward Island,
Canada
www.jobodesigns.com
www.jobodesigns.etsy.com
Ravelry: jobodesigns

Maggie Tipping
Westbrook, Maine
www.dispatchesfrommaine.com
Ravelry: Mags

Chris Morgan, with a few of her furry friends. This could be you! Not that I'm trying to influence you one way or the other...

Santa Fe, New Mexico
www.hareandthereproductions.com